AFFORDABLE ART DECO

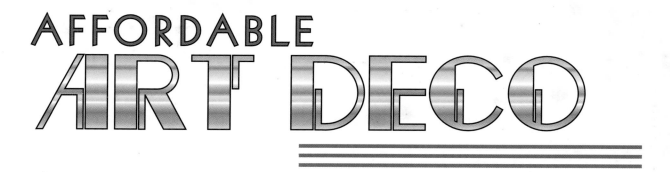

Identification & Value Guide

Hutchison
&
Johnson

COLLECTOR BOOKS

A Division of Schroeder Publishing Co., Inc.

The current values in this book should be used only as a guide. They are not intended to set prices, which vary from one section of the country to another. Auction prices as well as dealer prices vary greatly and are affected by condition as well as demand. Neither the authors nor the publisher assumes responsibility for any losses that might be incurred as a result of consulting this guide.

Searching for a Publisher?

We are always looking for knowledgeable people considered to be experts within their fields. If you feel that there is a real need for a book on your collectible subject and have a large comprehensive collection, contact Collector Books.

On the front cover, clockwise from top:
Decanter, maker unknown, $40.00; reverse painted tray, maker unknown, $350.00; streamline pen holder, $50.00 – 75.00; Evans cigarette box with removable pocket lighter (pictured here with wrong lighter), $300.00, with correct lighter, $400.00; Chase powder box, $20.00 – 35.00, perfect, $45.00 – 50.00.

Cover design:
Beth Summers

Book design:
Michelle Dowling

COLLECTOR BOOKS
P.O. Box 3009
Paducah, Kentucky 42002–3009

Copyright © 1999 by Ken Hutchison and Greg Johnson

Printed in the U.S.A. by Image Graphics, Paducah, KY

contents

Dedication 4

About the Author 4

Dedication 5

About the Photographer 5

Introduction 6

Slightly Sinful 10
      smoking 10
      drinking 22
      gambling 34

Setting Pretty — tableware 37

Vanity Fare — dressers & dresser sets 50

The World's Fair, 1933 – 1934 58

The Desk Set 63

Decoratives 73

Doing It All Deco 82

Everything's Coming Up Deco 101

dedication

To my mom and dad, who raised me in a Deco-free environment.

To my sister, Norma, and my friend, her husband, Ron, who share my passion for flea marketing.

To my mentor Nate Alexander who taught me so much without ever teaching — A really neat guy.

To Greg Johnson, professional photographer and friend, for his willingness to do this, our second book together. And for his patience and gentle good nature.

To all our pals at Volo Antique Mall just because they are our pals.

And, of course, to my friend Tom Huff for his understanding, enthusiasm, and cartoony sense of fun that made our pursuit of Art Deco so much fun. It has been a great pleasure growing up together.

— Ken Hutchison

about the author

Ken is a visual guy. Even his writing is visual. Small wonder that he was for years a creative director in a major Chicago advertising agency.

Ken has surrounded himself with visual treats. Classic cars, antique toys, art, sculpture, and, of course, Art Deco.

When we became acquainted he was just entering his Deco period. Our cultural common ground was the Beatles *Sergeant Pepper's Lonely Hearts Club Band.*

Soon I was his sidekick on all those exciting road trips to antique shows, flea markets, auctions, and weekend mall hopping. I met and enjoyed so many new people.

As my enthusisam for and understanding of things Deco grew — along with Ken's — our venture became a real partnership. It was fun. Laughs. Brats. And Ribs. And each new piece a visual delight.

But the high point came when we finished the fireplace, using porcelain panels from the very Deco Mercury Theater in Chicago. We shared a quiet evening of absolue awe. It was great.

And now I know and like cool jazz and the big bands, and Ken enjoys the Stones and even Frank Zappa.

Life with Ken is more than just a friendship. It is a visual experience.

—Tom Huff

dedication

In loving memory of my "Grandma T."
A most remarkable woman, she was an inspiration to all who knew her.

And to Meredith, my wife and my buddy.
And to our kids, Ben, Nick, David, and Little Nelly, who are growing up too fast. So many shoes, so little time.
And to Ken and Tom, just because they're Ken and Tom. Fun and Funny.

— Greg Johnson

about the photographer

Greg Johnson is a son, a father, my husband, and friend.

We have a place in rural Wisconsin with a horse or two, dogs that run off and get lost, chickens everywhere, and chores galore.

We love it here. And the kids have a ball. Greg grew up on a farm in South Dakota, so, to him, all this was a return to his roots.

To me, a city kid, it was a bit of culture shock at first. But before long, it was a return to nature. And for all the make-do or do-it-yourself situations that arise, I love the feelings of self-confidence that solving them has created.

Greg is a professional photographer. He sees everything — gets excited over the lights and shadows of sunrise and sunset. He sees the glow of the snow, whereas I see the shovel.

Life out here is challenging, but Greg takes on the many mini-crises with a sense of humor and endless good nature.

I guess I'll keep him.

— Meredith Johnson

introduction

If you like Art Deco...you *love* Art Deco. There's no halfway play. You are totally in tune with its simplicity, its elegance...and most of all, its devotion to the streamline design and materials of the 1930s, the *machine age.*

It was a time when the designers were at the forefront. The future was rushing toward us at astonishing speed. And it required designers of exceptional ability — given extraordinary freedom — to create "futurelook" and take future concepts to the market place. So delight after dazzling delight swept off their drawing boards as these designers put the face of the future on this decade of unparalleled progress.

However, the worldwide Depression coupled with the conservative nature of a threatened American middle class stood in the way of glorious success. And those reasons alone make Art Deco so difficult to find today.

Streamline paid dearly for that chilling expression, "what will the neighbors think?" A lot of the sleek chrome and black furnishings found their way into commercial service where they created a pleasing, exciting experience for those who couldn't quite dare to be different.

At home, the only Deco pieces frequently seen were radios and refrigerators. They were so new to the market place, one accommodated the appearance of newness. Many of the great industrial designers had radios and refrigerators on their resumés.

Several astonishing radios appeared in the slick publications of the time. The most striking being Walter Dorwin Teague's designs for Spartan Radio. A huge floor model was essentially a large round blue or peach mirror mounted on a chrome tubular frame. In the center was the tuner and speaker. Awesome. Similar table models were also available.

But such delicacies as these were far too radical for Waterloo, Iowa. Or Chicago or New York for that matter. They were for the avant garde on Michigan Avenue or Fifth Avenue. Maybe more likely, in Miami and Beverly Hills where so very much was new — and the wealthy and adventurous were the settlers in these new frontiers.

For the folks in middle America dealing cautiously with hard times, Deco designs were given as wedding gifts to the young at heart. Elegant decanters, candy dishes, cigarette boxes, and chic lighters from Chase, Manning Bowman, various Farbers, Ronson, and Elgin were graciously given. And often put lovingly away to be treasured out of sight for the next 50 years. Coffee makers and tea service sets were the next higher level.

And today, these gifts are the basics of affordable elegance from the Art Deco period.

However, for the collector or home decorator who is willing to take the time, and exhibit remarkable patience, there is a wealth of awesome design out there for the not-so-wealthy Deco lover.

ART DECO DEFINED

The expression Art Deco means different things to different people. It wasn't even called Art Deco when it became a machine age trend. Apparently, that name was applied in the 1960s.

It began to be recognized in France in 1925 with the Exposition des Arts Decoratifs. But it was ill-defined, covering as it did an enormous expanse of design concepts. The factor that was to have tied it all together was a sense of simplicity — a lack of superfluous decoration that usually festooned traditional furnishings.

Yet in many books about Art Deco, they feature the most costly, rarest European works in which exotic veneers, imaginative design, and very limited availability established them as landmarks. But for the most part, they were not the design milestones they are puffed up to be.

Worse, the reader will not find the name of a single American designer. And virtually everything shown would be something Sotheby's would be interested in selling — items with a pedigree; boasting rights for the very wealthy. But for our purposes, they tend to leave Art Deco undefined.

Our definition: Art Deco is determined by its progressive design, its simplicity, and its use of

machine age materials. Steel or brass plated with chromium. Plastics like Bakelite, and the more colorful Catalin, which had the heft and feel of ivory and were just as hard. Natural materials were used, but wood was often painted as if it were steel. Leathers were rarely used in natural colors. Leatherette helped mass producers keep costs in line. And much of the finest design was also distinctive because it was so affordable.

In Europe, Marcel Breuer broke ground with the Wassily chair. Mies Van der Rohe created a timeless classic with the Barcelona chair. LeCorbusier's Grand Confort chair and couch designs of 1928 were sensational. All three of these creations are still being produced today.

In America, the Deco period was the *dawn of design.* And the golden age of the designer.

Today, the only designers anyone can name are in the clothing business. High fashion reputations riding around on the seats of blue jeans and the tags of underpants.

But in the 1930s, the names of great designers appeared everywhere. Norman Bel Geddes, Donald Deskey, Raymond Loewy, Walter Dorwin Teague, Gilbert Rohde, Paul Frankl, Wolfgang Hoffman, Kem Weber, Walter Von Nessen...the list goes on and on.

They created chairs, couches, clocks, cars, cameras, coffee makers, and carafes — and that's just some of the "C's." How about houses, theatres, locomotives, decanters, lamps, bedrooms, bars, dishes, silver services, and myriad appliances. From 1930 to 1940 was the decade of design. And American designers were to the 30s what Italian designers were to the 50s — international celebrities.

SIN...AND ART DECO

Art Deco was too much for mom's parlor or dining room. But it was okay for things sinful. Liquor, cigarettes, and gambling were comfortable ways to enjoy Deco accessories in a traditional environment. They made special moments even more special.

After all, in 1933, Prohibition came to a halt just as the machine age was really rolling. Social drinking was in again and Art Deco tools helped make it an elegant ritual.

William Powell and Myrna Loy played a role in creating *martini glamour* — and the desire to share in the sophistication of it.

Cigarettes were chic then. And cigarette cases, servers, lighters, and ashtrays were often real doozies. Deco style was high gear among those who smoked as a matter of fashion.

And gambling. Some wonderfully inventive poker chip carriers graced the Saturday night games. And beautiful Catalin carriers and chips gave a game a sense of grace.

Deco design gave permission to sin...so long as it was done with style. That touch of elegance and sense of ritual took much of the curse off such pursuits.

ART DECO — SUCCESS OR FAILURE?

The American *streamline* era we call Art Deco was a marriage between the unlikely bedfellows of industry and fine art.

Yet throughout a decade which changed the face of a nation...a decade in which "the future" was explored, designed, and presented for sale...the twin powers of a devastating Depression and a very conservative public doomed *the dawn of design* to commercial failure.

People loved looking at streamline. The Chicago World's Fair in 1933 — *A Century of Progress* — was a Deco feast for those who attended, and those with whom they shared the souvenirs back home.

In the movies Deco was the very definition of high style. Indeed, the theater itself may well have provided an evening's experience in Deco elegance. Beauty shops delighted fashion conscious patrons with the glittering glamour of Art Deco designs.

But at home, in this time of hard times, most people lived with what they had. And when something new was called for, it had to fit in. A Kem Weber triple tube couch in our house would have looked like a Martian had landed in the living room.

That was the problem. Simply put...in home decoration, Art Deco was an all or nothing-at-all proposition. And most people couldn't afford to redo the whole house...or even the entire bedroom...so they were left to enjoy Deco in other venues.

Today, Art Deco mixes quite well with other modern styles. And it often provides refreshing accents that delight and excite the senses.

Art Deco represents a time when the future was something a person could see and touch and feel deep inside. And today, it says in a bold voice "look at me...I'm here...the future is back."

ART DECO VALUE GUIDE

The prices in this book are based on prices we've actually paid, prices we've seen at shows, prices realized at our place.

Naturally, with most of these items, we give a value range from low to high, depending on condition and location. New York and the West

8

Coast demand substantially higher prices than other parts of the country.

ART DECO SHOPPING GUIDE

Now, just a few comments about shopping for Art Deco.

Many Art Deco accessories are such a bargain that most dealers are doing it as a labor of love. Only when a dealer makes a great buy, can he or she realize a healthy profit.

~~~~~~

At the best shows and twentieth century auctions, higher prices are demanded or bid up...and paid by people who really don't have the time or the inner drive to go out looking for the best deal. They pay more, and yet probably come out money ahead. We could call them the smartest buyers.

Even though they pay more, they get exactly what they want.

~~~~~~

At lesser shows and run-of-the-mill auctions, there may be "deals." And yet, you may discover later, it isn't really what you wanted. It just looked like such a good deal at the time.

Plus you may put in hours waiting for your item to come up for bids. And you risk bidding on other "bargains" you end up selling, just because you became swept up in auction action.

The lesser shows can be fun outings if you can keep your adrenaline in check. Racing around to get everywhere first is exhausting and unproductive. Try to remember that everyone you see is not looking for Art Deco. Most wouldn't take it on a bet. So enjoy the day.

BUYING FROM DECO DEALERS

When you go to a twentieth century show, get cards from the dealers and make notes on the back indicating their specialties. Remember, it isn't easy being a Deco dealer. Deco is hard to find, and it's a very small segment of the antique market.

Form relationships with the better dealers. And don't try to beat their brains out on price. If you treat them right, they will notify you when they find what you're looking for. Remember, they're taking all the risks, paying a lot of overhead and travel costs. And presenting you with high quality choices.

And remember this: Most dealers will reward repeat customers with a discount if they can. If you treat your favorite dealers like friends — better yet, become friends — they will not only turn you on to the best affordable Deco, they will also help keep you from making costly mistakes.

When you make a great buy on some Deco you really don't want, take it to your Deco dealer. But don't try to make a killing on it. Remember the dealer has a lot of overhead to pay, and can't afford to give you anything near what he or she will ask for it.

Buying Art Deco is a long term passion. The search is half the fun of it. So easy does it...walk, don't run, smell the bratwurst, and have a good time.

You'll come out of it all surrounded by the things you've wanted, having enjoyed the experience of doing it.

And you'll have gained some wonderful friendships along the way.

slightly sinful

smoking —

Today, it's as out of fashion as it was chic in the 1930s. For men, it was a matter of manliness. For women, the very symbol of sophistication. And, for women, it was far more ritualistic. For men, more matter of fact.

But for the gentleman, it was an opportunity to impress with a sense of style and an air of elegance.

All this required paraphernalia. And Deco design was the hallmark of smoking with grace. Lighters, cigarette cases, and ashtrays afforded the smoker the opportunity to turn a "filthy, nasty habit" into an almost artistic expression of one's good taste.

And women of fashion were encouraged to reach for a cigarette instead of a sweet. Who knew?

TABLE LIGHTERS

They afforded a touch of elegance for the smart set.
Today, they're not so affordable. But by design, many
of them practically define machine age Art Deco.

top:
RONSON MODEL 2110 TOUCH TIP
"STREAMLINED." The definitive Art Deco
table lighter, it was available in black and
tortoise as shown, and also in white. This
Ronson design is my personal favorite.
$250.00 – 400.00.

right:
Left: RONSON TOUCH-TIP DELUXE.
Rather traditional in style and proportion,
but Deco in the details. $150.00 –
225.00. Right: RONSON TOUCH-TIP
LIGHTER AND WATCH COMBO. This
was a bright idea — and so expressive of
machine age thinking. Why should something useful in one way not be useful in two
ways? $225.00 – 300.00.

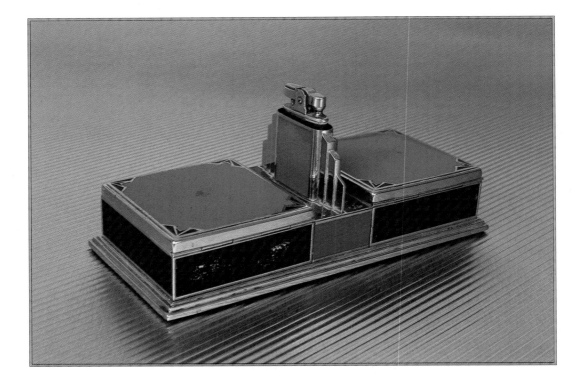

top:

EVANS CIGARETTE
BOX WITH REMOVABLE
POCKET LIGHTER.
Another bright idea...but.
The pocket lighter always
got lost. But what a beautiful Deco design and bril-
liant color. The lighter here
is the wrong one of course.
$300.00. With correct
lighter, $400.00.

left:

Left: RONSON "SPAR-
TAN" TABLE LIGHTER.
Very machine age. Very
handsome. This lighter
was also very popular.
$35.00 – 50.00.
Right: GREEN CATALIN
TABLE LIGHTER. For the
Catalin lover's table.
$45.00 – 60.00.

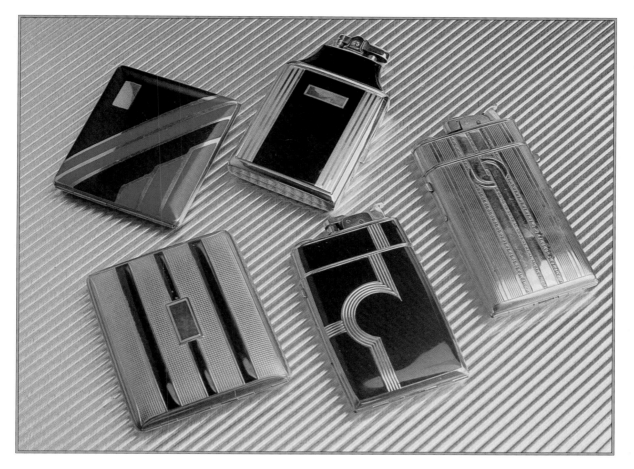

Center top: RONSON LIGHTER AND CIGARETTE CASE. $25.00 – 35.00.

Center bottom: EVANS LIGHTER AND CASE IN BLACK AND CHROME. $30.00 – 40.00.

Right: EVANS LIGHTER IN BRUSHED CHROME. $25.00 – 35.00.

Upper left: BLACK AND RED CIGARETTE CASE. No maker identification. $15.00 – 20.00.

Lower left: BLACK AND SILVER CIGARETTE CASE. $20.00 – 25.00.

ASHTRAYS

They were an important element of home or office decor. It was expected that guests would be smokers. Among those who perceived themselves as avant garde, smoking was elevated to a fine art. Chic and actively ritualistic.

An elegant cigarette holder may have been a bit eccentric for most who smoked as a matter of fashion. But having the oh-so-right ashtrays in the home was a telling expression of self-confident individuality.

And the most gracious among them were those ashtrays that were self-cleaning. An ashtray full of butts was not sophistication.

STANDING ASHTRAYS —

top right:
HIS AND HERS FLOOR ASHTRAYS. These handsome drum-inspired ashtrays are glamorously Art Deco. Push a lever and the contents disappear into the base. Neat, huh. The small one on triple tubes was the choice of Barbra Streisand for her Art Deco environment. The cream/tan is especially rich. His $80.00. Hers $40.00 – 70.00.

left:
SMOKER'S CABINET. Painted black with strong chrome accents, this was designed to stand guard beside the favored chair of the gentleman of the house. Smoking items could be stowed out of sight. So could the butts at the touch of a button. Ideal for the pipe smoker. And little flip-up tables on each side were on hand for the cocktail hour. Oh my. Condition matters. $125.00 – 225.00.

slightly sinful

top right:

UNHOLY ROLLER ASHTRAY. These are so neat. Just grab the top and roll it to where it is needed. Let go and it rights itself. A must for "the club." And today, it's just fun. Condition and color are of paramount importance. $125.00 – 300.00.

left:

ASHTRAY TABLE WITH STORAGE AREA. This handsome ashtray table in black and chrome features three sliding panels in the drum section. Ideal for storing smoking stuff, a pad and pencil, well, you name it. It is a handsome Deco design. Quite striking and very practical. The ashtray is self-emptying, too. $125.00 – 140.00.

lower left:

SHIPBOARD ASHTRAY TABLE. These are hard to find complete. They are designed to fold when not in use. As they unfolded, the tips of the legs slipped under clips on deck, holding the table secure. $200.00 – 300.00.

lower right:

ROUND TWO-TIER ASHTRAY TABLE. A charming color for a most convenient kind of ashtray table. Self-cleaning, of course. And plenty of room for the cocktail hour. Even a shelf to store the bottles. $100.00 – 150.00.

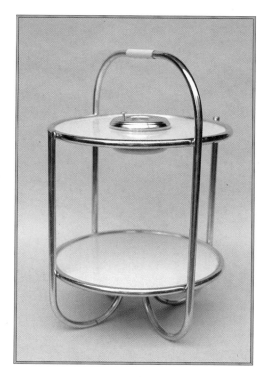

left:

CLIMAX COCKTAIL SMOKER. Designed by W. J. Campbell, this has become a true Deco classic. Extremely well made and properly weighted, it is easy to disassemble and clean. But mostly, it dazzles with the brilliance of its design. $250.00 – 300.00.

bottom left:

BLACK AND CHROME STRAP ASH TABLE. What an elegant design. The top is heavy duty Bakelite. The chrome straps are bold to the point of daring. I bought this at a serious auction and went there determined to get it. Just one of those things. $400.00 – 650.00.

bottom right:

Left: STAINLESS STEEL AND BRASS. The combination of metal colors makes this ashtray attractive. The brass was badly tarnished when we bought it, so we polished one brass tube and left the other tarnished to add a third color. $60.00 – 75.00. Right: SKY-SCRAPER-TYPE ASHTRAY. The slender bow supports with their very Deco chrome trim give this ashtray a moderne appearance. In brass finish and painted in red and cream. These seem rather commercial, like for office or beauty shop use. Painted, $75.00 – 90.00. Brass, $85.00 – 125.00.

LIGHTED ASHTRAYS —

Using colorful art glass, the manufacturers of lighted ashtrays produced a prodigious number of designs. There's little point in showing a lot of them, because even then we'd only be scratching the surface. Find one you like, and buy it. Simple as that. But they're fun. You can change the color by putting in a different Christmas tree bulb. Note: we use ours as night lights.

left:
AIRPLANE LIGHTED ASHTRAY. There is always an exception to the rule. In the case of lighted ashtrays, this is the one. With the Lockheed Hudson on top, its value takes off. Landing one of these babies isn't as easy as you might wish. $400.00 – 500.00+.

right:
PAIR OF ART GLASS LIGHTED ASHTRAYS. These are especially showy. Lights in both the base and the top. As a general rule, lighted ashtrays run from $75.00 to 125.00 in good condition, and with all their parts. $125.00 – 150.00 each.

TABLE ASHTRAYS —

left:

CHROME AND FROSTED GLASS ASH-
TRAY. Frosted glass and chrome set the
stage, but the four chrome spheres put on
the show in this handsome machine age
Deco ashtray. $30.00 – 40.00.

bottom left:

MANNING-BOWMAN CHROME BALL.
This is one of my favorites. So simple. So
Deco. $35.00 – 50.00. CHASE
ARISTOCRAT ASHTRAY. Another elegant
design. Very much machine age. Available
in chrome on brass, polished brass, or smoke
and brass. $35.00 – 50.00.

bottom center:

Background: CHASE GLOBE ASHTRAY.
Just flip the lid closed and cigarette butts are
extinguished by shutting off the supply of
oxygen. Nice idea. But not quite so easy to
do. $30.00 – 45.00. Foreground:
CHASE CHROME STACKING ASH-
TRAYS. Very nicely streamlined, but not
very practical. Minimal capacity. Set of
four, $30.00 – 45.00.

bottom right:

THE COMMODORE ASHTRAY. A pleasing
design of a very practical ashtray. Just pull
up on the ball and the contents would fall into
the black ball. Releasing the ball oxygen-
starves any smoldering stuff, putting it out.
Made by the Novelty Division of Danbury
Electric Mfg. Co. $25.00 – 40.00.

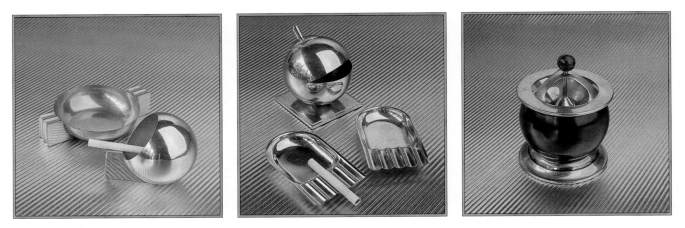

CIGARETTE BOXES

Among the more sophisticated circles, having a cigarette box on the side table and the office desk was the mark of grace and thoughtful consideration of the needs or desires of a guest.

Manners and the rituals of etiquette were in vogue in the 1930s. During those hard times, one could adapt some of the affectations regularly seen in the movies.

So while everything was done on a budget... it cost nothing to be polite.

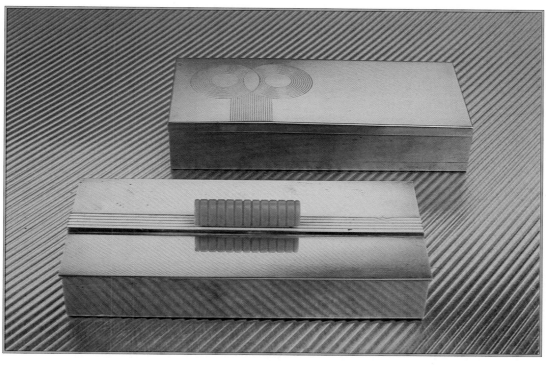

top right:
CHASE COSMOPOLITAN CIGARETTE BOX. A tasteful little box, yet the design conceals the pretty Bakelite base. $45.00 – 60.00.
above:
Background: CHASE BRASS CIGARETTE BOX. Chase featured a wide variety of cigarette box designs, many which we have not found cataloged. Most are elegant and probably are of roughly equal value. It becomes just a matter of taste. Virtually all Chase products are marked somewhere. $40.00 – 55.00. Foreground: CHASE BRASS AND WHITE BOX WITH BAKELITE HANDLE. Again, elegant simplicity. Chase hired excellent design consultants. $40.00 – 55.00.

top left:

CHROME-PLATED CIGARETTE BOX. This came as a set: cigarette box, two matchbox holders, and two ashtrays. It is most attractive in the right setting. $65.00 – 85.00.

middle left:

LACQUERED WOOD BOX. The lacquered finish is applied in geometric patterns ala Mondrian, in silver and red against a background of walnut. $30.00 – 40.00. May well be found for less.

middle right:

SQUARE BOX IN CHROME AND CREAM. $35.00 – 55.00.

bottom:

THREE ROLLTOP CIGARETTE BOXES. These rolltops are really quite a delight — pleasing to the eye and a pleasure to use, probably these days for small jewelry or desk items. Be sure the rolltop is in excellent condition. Examine carefully for cracks. Square Rolltop in Red and Black. $35.00 – 45.00. Oval Rolltop in Red and Black. $35.00 – 45.00. Double Oval Rolltop in Red and Black. $35.00 – 45.00.

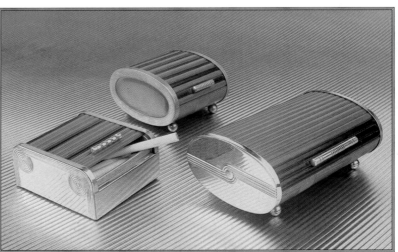

top right:
CHROME AND BLACK UPRIGHT CIGARETTE BOX. Slim and trim, this very unusual model contains cigarettes on either side — rather like an early toaster. Turn the lever on top, and the side panels drop down, delivering cigarettes in style. $40.00 – 60.00.

bottom left:
PULL-UP CIGARETTE DISPENSER. These were made for years and years. But the early ones, like this, had a Catalin barrel and top pull. And they're very attractive. Later editions with a variety of decoration on the barrel probably aren't worth collecting. $60.00 – 100.00.

bottom right:
CHROME AND RED CIGARETTE BOX. A very fresh design. $20.00 – 30.00.

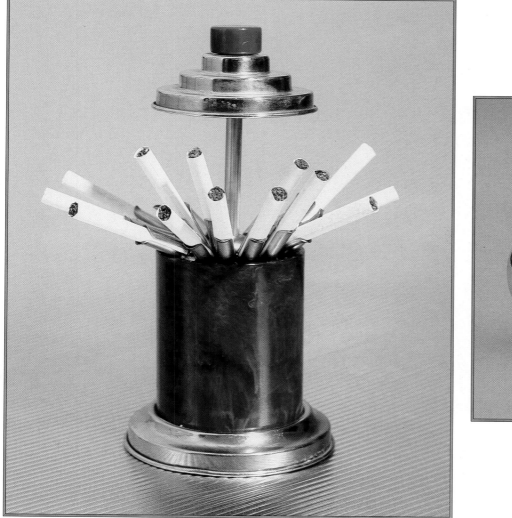

drinking —

Mixing drinks for guests was a matter of considerable care. It was important to know one's way around the home bar in these post-Prohibition times.

Contrary to many a dire prediction of the time, people didn't simply drink bourbon from the bottle until stupor set in. Rather, they took pleasure in a new kind of hosting.

And the artists of Art Deco designed everything it took to make mixing drinks appear to be a mixture of male expertise, an expression of high art, and more than a little showmanship.

Maybe, showoffmanship. It was a wonderful display of ritual sophistication.

previous page and this page:

WIDE ANGLE BAR BY BEAUTILITY. An ultimate in home bars, this work of art, by Beautility of England, makes me laugh every time I open it. An elaborate mechanical system is unleashed as the front is pulled down. The sides swing out automatically, revealing a cornucopia of glassware, bottles, bar tools, and a mirrored working surface. And the light goes on. It's incredible. And what fun it must have been to amaze and delight one's friends with such a flamboyant entry to an evening ritual. Nick and Nora Charles would be proud. $1,250.00 – 1,500.00.

above left and right:
ROTARY CENTER BAR. A product of England,
this bar features a display area on top for glassware
and twin display areas on either side for additional
paraphernalia. The magic is in the center — a
beautiful column design covered in copper/gold mir-
rors. Just rotate it to the right, and — *voila!* — it
reveals two hitherto concealed liquor bottles. The last
owner never knew the secret compartment was there.
No kidding. $500.00 – 700.00.

right:

DISPLAY TOP BAR. Another example from England, this time by Sureline, features a convex lower portion and concave upper. The sliding glass is also curved. It includes a pullout work area with gold striped mirrored glass, and in the upper section a base of the same mirroring with a back panel mirror featuring palm trees and floating drink things. $500.00 – 700.00.

below left:

TABLE TOP BAKELITE BAR. This is movie star stuff. It just looks right. We see these every so often. $125.00 – 175.00.

bottom:

STREAMLINE TABLE TOP BAR. In stainless steel and walnut, this table top bar has a machine age quality right down to the balls of its feet. $100.00 – 150.00.

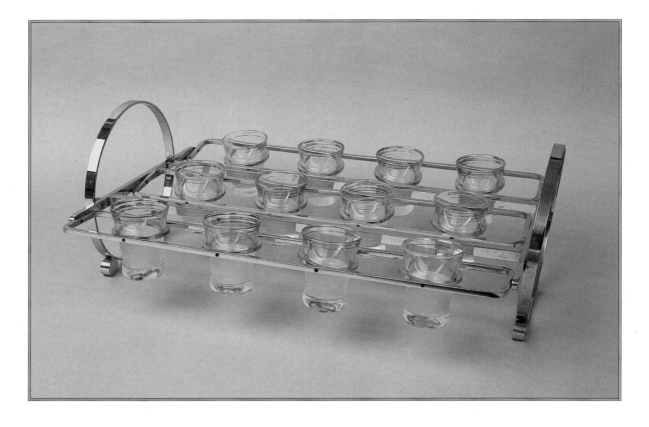

above:
SHIPBOARD BAR GLASSES SET.
Designed to make the glasses roll with the ship, so they wouldn't slide away and break. Very Deco. $300.00 – 400.00.

left:
BARSIDE REFRIGERATOR-FREEZER.
Manufactured by Freeze Pak, the small capacity refrigerator-freezer is a radical streamline design. The legs are most unexpected. And the large circular door openings are dramatically Deco. It's almost a caricature of modern design. Everybody loves it. Everybody! Note: The prices these in similar condition have brought at auctions and twentieth century shows vary widely. $900.00 – 2,500.00.

COCKTAIL SHAKERS

CHASE GAITY COCKTAIL SHAKER. Chase made what many consider the most beautiful decanter on the mass market with the Gaity cocktail shaker. Most beautiful and certainly most plentiful, as it was a popular gift item in the post-Prohibition 30s. This accounts for its modest prices today. Be sure to buy the very best you can find. THE CHASE ICE BUCKET. A companion piece to the Gaity cocktail shaker — used here as a vase — is much harder to find. Gaity Cocktail Shaker with two cups, $40.00 – 65.00. Complete set with four cups and tray, $65.00 – 95.00. Matching Ice Bucket, $65.00 – 80.00.

above left:
CHASE GAITY SHAKER IN CHROME AND WHITE. This rarer version of the Gaity cocktail shaker featured white trim rings. $70.00.

above middle:
CHASE TARGET COCKTAIL SHAKER. It has a tall look. A simple cylinder, it is adorned with a great many parallel lines. The lid was available in ivory and dark blue. $60.00 – 80.00.

above right:
DOUBLE-HANDLED COCKTAIL TWIRLER. Grab one Lucite handle in each hand and let 'er rip. Just the trick for guests who like their martinis not shaken or stirred, but swirled. $125.00 – 175.00.

above left:
SKYSCRAPER BY REVERE. This may be the most desired of the cocktail shakers. And the most expensive. Designed by Norman Bel Geddes, it soars above others in dramatic expression of its name. The cups, which are not shown, are even more desirable. And the tray on which it is sitting — the Manhattan tray — is sought for its own sake. Skyscraper, $400.00 – 800.00. Manhattan Tray, $175.00 – 250.00.

above right:
CHROME CYLINDER WITH STREAMLINE TRIM BY MANNING-BOWMAN. $40.00 – 50.00.

right:
Left: CHROME CYLINDER WITH BLACK BAKELITE TRIM. $35.00 – 45.00. Right: CHROME CYLINDER WITH WALNUT TRIM BY MANNING-BOWMAN. $35.00 – 45.00.

far left:
CHROME CYLINDER WITH BLACK HORIZONTAL STRIPES BY EVERCRAFT. A slimmer expression of the Chase Gaity design. Simple. Elegant. $45.00 – 65.00.

left:
DRAMATIC TAPERED DECANTER. An interesting feature is the display of recipes on the bottom. $45.00 – 65.00.

above & left:
BRANDY PUMP WITH SIX GLASSES INSIDE CHROME BALL. $45.00 – 65.00.

clockwise beginning from top left:

CHROME VESSEL WITH SIX MATCHING MUGS HANGING ON THE SIDES. $60.00 – 80.00.

CHROME BOTTLE WITH RED CATALIN TRIM AND SIX HANGING GLASSES. $70.00 – 90.00.

BRANDY PUMP MOUNTED ON GLASS HORS D'OUVRES TRAY. $60.00 – 80.00.

BRANDY PUMP WITH FOUR ETCHED GLASSES ON TRAY. $65.00 – 85.00.

left:
FROSTED GLASS CORDIAL DECANTER WITH FOUR GOBLETS. Girls, girls, girls, girls. Very Vargas. $100.00 – 150.00.

below left:
ICE BUCKET BY MANNING-BOWMAN. Chrome with butterscotch Catalin trim. An elegant design. So fine. $120.00 – 150.00.

below right:
ICE BUCKET BY REVERE WITH CATALIN SPIRE. Attributed to Norman Bel Geddes, it is a rare and inspiring design. $150.00 – 225.00.

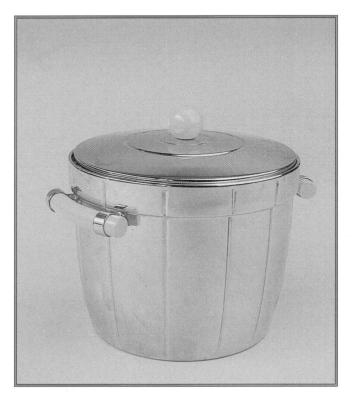

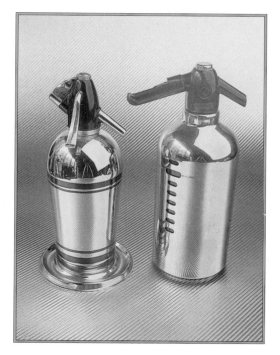

clockwise beginning from top left:

ICE BUCKET. Polished aluminum with maroon Catalin handles. $45.00 – 60.00.

ICE BUCKET. Polished aluminum and black plastic by Kromex. $25.00 – 35.00.

CHAMPAIGN CHILLER. Huge pewter penguin. Made in Italy. Of the many intriguing things in our house, this commands the most interest among our guests. $350.00+.

Right: SODA KING SODA SPRITZER. Gives visual measure of contents. Excellent and working, $50.00. Not working, $20.00. Left: SODA SPRITZER BY SPARKLETS OF ENGLAND. Chrome and black with small tray. $50.00 – 70.00.

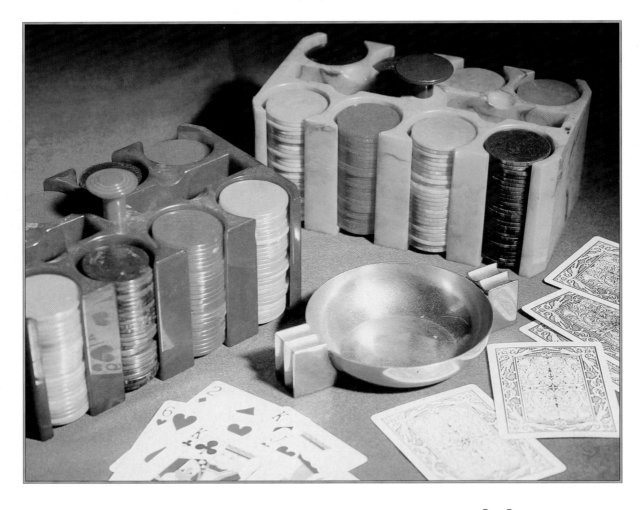

gambling ——

During the Deco era, a popular form of entertainment for men was the poker game.

Men formed close-knit clubs and played cards on the same night every week.

Women followed suit, holding regular events for the bridge club.

The poker game was generally a low stakes affair. And considerable attention was paid to the accoutrements. The chips, ashtrays, drink preparation, and snacks served with grace by the virtually invisible wife.

It was ritual, as last seen on television in the home of Oscar Madison and Felix Unger. But done the way Felix would have wanted it.

right:
CATALIN POKER CHIP CADDIES. Just the thing for collectors who regard Catalin as a semi-precious gem. Intensely satisfying. So smooth and slick and solid. A tactile delight. A visual dessert. We've seen them in butterscotch, maroon, green, and lipstick red. One of my favorite things. $200.00 – 275.00 each. Right: SMALL BUTTERSCOTCH CATALIN CADDY. Round with Catalin chips. $45.00 – 65.00.

Note: Often the caddy and chips can be found separately. You'll probably save a little money, but more important you'll enjoy the satisfaction of building your complete set.

bottom left:
BOXED SET OF CATALIN CHIPS. Contains six chip holders with three rows of chips in each and two decks of never-unwrapped old playing cards. The Catalin chips are awesome in peach/tangerine, aqua, and lavender colors. The box itself is nothing special. $100.00 – 135.00.

bottom right:
STACKABLE BAKELITE INDIVIDUAL POKER CHIP AND COASTER TRAYS. Catalin chips. A touch of class for the middle class. $50.00.

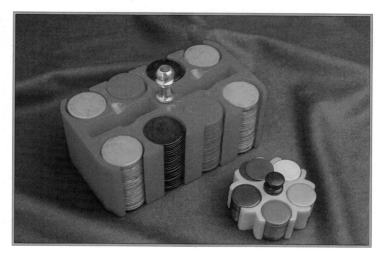

top left:

BROWN BAKELITE CHIP CADDY/DISPENSER. The Count-Rite Company created a winning hand with their remarkable chip counting dispenser. It selects the number of chips for each player, without having to actually count them. Neat, huh? $135.00 – 195.00.

top right:

TURN-IT CHIP CADDY. A remarkable piece of machine age invention. Turn the handle on the top — presto! — the tubes of chips swing grandly out. A terrific idea and stunning design by Turnit Mfg. Co. $140.00 – 200.00.

right:
FOUR SUITS NUT DISHES. Or are they for bridge mix candies? Well, hearts, diamonds, clubs, or spades — take your pick. These show up often in nice condition. They were just too small for any good use. Simple gifts that ended up in a drawer somewhere. $15.00 – 20.00.

setting pretty

tableware —

In those hard times of the Depression 30s, small luxuries took on deeper meaning. Neighbors and friends gathered in each other's homes, and whether for simple dining or just cocktails, it was more pleasurable to do it in style.

Perhaps if we glance back at our youth…our early 20s, we can recall the delight we took in little treasures. Now that we can afford so much more — and because we know so much more — it takes a whole lot more to have such lovely moments of pure pleasure.

The 1930s provided a panoply of simple elegances, visual treats, created by top designers, at affordable prices.

And for those who had so little, little things meant a lot.

COFFEE SERVICES AND TEA SETS

top left:
CHASE DIPLOMAT COFFEE SERVICE. This is probably my favorite design. Simple. Deco. Rather formal. Very elegant. The fluted surfaces play with candlelight delightfully. $300.00+.

top right:
FARBER COFFEE SERVICE IN CHROME AND LUCITE. It wouldn't be exceptional except for the Lucite handles on the creamer and sugar. These delightful discs with a bite taken out of them make the ordinary extraordinary. $100.00 – 125.00.

left:
CHASE CONTINENTAL COFFEE SERVICE. The epitome of Deco concepts expressed with traditional elegance. Chase designers had a remarkable sense of style that defines Deco streamline with dignity and grace. $100.00 – 175.00.

FLUTED COFFEE SERVICE. Apparently German, it has both German and French material descriptions on the bottom. Matching large and medium size tea kettles are also available. The design is simply beautiful. Fluted Coffee Service, $125.00 – 175.00. Matching Tea Kettles, $35.00 – 50.00 each.

FARBER BROTHERS TEA SET WITH IVORY BAKELITE HANDLES. These sets by Farber, with their lovely Bakelite handles, are very impressive. They are not distinguished Deco designs, but the materials make up for that. $75.00 – 90.00.

TEAPOT BY MANNING-BOWMAN. Flamboyant with its huge Catalin handle, squatting stance, and ball-bearing base, it is as daring as it is elegant. Hey, it works! $100.00 – 150.00.

ELECTRIC COFFEE MAKERS

The most important thing is, "Does it work?" It must. Check to be sure the inside parts are there as well as the cord. However, new cords can be obtained and it may be the safe thing to do. Many of the coffee makers were wedding gifts — too fancy for everyday use — and may never have been used at all. In most instances, everyday cups are too tall to fit under the spigots, making them awkward and rather dangerous to use.

top left:
ELECTRIC COFFEE MAKER BY FARBER BROS., KROME KRAFT. $55.00 – 70.00.

bottom left:
MANNING BOWMAN COFFEE SPHERE. Oh, these look so right. Dramatic. Daring. Delightfully Deco. They should cost a whole lot more than they do. $60.00 – 100.00.

above:
COMET COFFEE SERVICE BY CHASE. This is a favorite of collectors. The design is outstanding. It is also rather difficult to obtain. However, some of the pieces individually show up for peanuts. If you see the creamer cheap, buy it. Same with the sugar. We've pieced together a couple complete sets this way, and have elegant creamers and sugars we can use everyday. Otherwise, this set is pricey. We've also included the matching non-electric teapot, because they all look so nice together. $275.00 – 350.00. Teapot, $100.00 – 125.00.

right:

CERAMIC ELECTRIC COFFEE SERVICE BY HEAT MASTER. This is the only ceramic set I've seen that is truly Deco in design. Fired in ivory with silver speed lines, it combines the brittle nature of streamline styling with the softer coloring of ceramic. Just right. $125.00 – 175.00.

middle left:

PERCOLATOR SERVICE WITH TRAY BY MANNING BOWMAN. Rather too formal, this coffee service with tray is virtually unused. The use of lipstick red Catalin trim is terrific. $85.00 – 125.00.

bottom left:

PERCOLATOR SERVICE WITH TRAY BY UNIVERSAL. Like new. But less spectacular with its white Bakelite trim. $65.00 – 85.00.

bottom right:

SUNBEAM COFFEE WARMER WITH SUGAR, CREAMER, AND TRAY. What's missing is the heating element it sits on. We just haven't found one yet. This is a rather common set. Yet the design is very Deco. $50.00 – 75.00.

SUGARS and CREAMERS

top left:
STREAMLINE SUGAR AND CREAMER WITH TRAY. There is no mark to identify the manufacturer. Too bad. They should have been particularly proud of this set for its daring purity of design. $100.00 – 150.00.

middle left:
CHASE SATURN SUGAR AND CREAMER. What a pretty little set. How "Chase" of them. It is so right. $40.00 – 65.00.

bottom left & right:
MANNING-BOWMAN SIDE BY SIDE SUGAR AND CREAMER. I just love this one. What a clever bit of design. Perhaps not the right idea for a restrained 1930s home. But S'wonderful. S'marvelous. $55.00 – 75.00.

top:
MANNING-BOWMAN SUGAR AND CREAMER.
$45.00 – 50.00.

middle:
ENGLISH SUGAR AND CREAMER.
$45.00 – 55.00.

right:
CHROME WITH BLACK BAKELITE DISC
HANDLES. What a nice piece of design. No
hallmark. Expression Deco. $50.00 – 70.00.

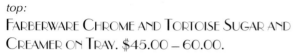

top:

FARBERWARE CHROME AND TORTOISE SUGAR AND
CREAMER ON TRAY. $45.00 – 60.00.

right & below:

FARBERWARE STACKABLE SUGAR AND CREAMER. Invention
during the Deco/machine age period was inspired by freedom and
imagination. Necessity was not always its mother. This Farberware
stackable sugar and creamer is a case in point. It sure looks like a
nifty idea, until the hostess tries to use it. As it's being unstacked, it
unloads. The sugar…the cream…the works. $35.00 – 50.00.

right & below:
CHASE STACKABLE BREAKFAST SET.
Chase came out with something even prettier…and sillier. Hot coffee or tea on the bottom — one cup. Cream in the middle. Sugar on top. Even Nora Charles, breakfasting grandly in bed, would have made a grand mess with this outfit. Nonetheless, it is a striking addition to any Deco collection. Just don't use it. $60.00 – 85.00.

left:

STREAMLINE PITCHER/COCKTAIL SERVER. It delivered machine age/Deco design to the max. Just imagine this pitcher on the bridge table with the Chase canape set. The picture clearly shows the delightful detail that promised a better world tomorrow. $100.00 – 125.00.

below:

MANNING-BOWMAN SYRUP SERVER. It looks like an overgrown creamer with no sugar bowl. No wonder it was passed over for a long time, according to the dealer. Like all Manning-Bowman designs, it has grace and style. The little tray is the clue to its use. Who wants a gooey table cloth after the waffles are gone? $35.00.

SPECIAL SERVING PIECES

top:

CHASE ELECTRIC SNACK SERVER. This lovely round server kept food hot by heating water in the base. An elegant way to serve a buffet. These are highly regarded for their design and they are on special occasion, very useful today. $150.00 – 250.00.

middle:

CHASE ELECTRIC BUFFET SERVER. With four rather large ceramic serving bowls, this was designed for the hostess who served the mostest. They are quite hard to find. They work great. But before you buy, examine the base unit for fatigue cracks. Large Chase pieces often have developed them. We found both of our servers at an antique flea market. One for $8.00. The other for $10.00. These can be found at bargain prices because most people don't recognize them as collectible, but regard them as discarded catering hardware. $200.00 – 300.00.

bottom:

CHASE CANAPE PLATE AND CHASE CUP. Original cost $1.50. Very much high style. Very affordable. And at the bridge table...very gracious. Very impressive. Few women worked outside the home in the 1930s and the afternoon bridge game was a familiar social gathering. And a sort of competition among hostesses as to who made the nicest luncheon or snack presentation. It was a time when families short on money were nevertheless long on manners. $60.00. Set of four, $250.00.

47

top:

Three Cocktail Delights. Left: CHASE COCKTAIL BALL. Before guests arrive, the hostess puts a decorous toothpick in each hole on the ball. Guests help themselves to the toothpicks and to the cocktail wieners or shrimp. $40.00 – 50.00. Center: FLAMINGO COCKTAIL BIRD. These show up frequently. Often the silver plate is peeling or worse. But a good one is still cute and quirky. $20.00 – 30.00. Right: COCKTAIL TURTLE. Well, why not a turtle? On the other hand, why a turtle? $12.00 – 16.00.

middle:

CHASE SALAD SERVERS. Designed for a young couple's "salad days," the Chase serving set combines excellent design with beautiful color. $50.00 – 75.00.

bottom:

MANNING BOWMAN RELISH SERV-ER AND TRAY. The glass is deeply engraved and frosted with Deco pattern. It is fitted to a chrome tray. The chrome lid features a serrated design. And, what luck, the spoon was still with it. $45.00 – 60.00.

top right:

CHASE LOTUS SAUCE BOWL. $35.00 – 40.00.

middle right:

CHASE VIKING GRAVY BOAT. $35.00 – 50.00.

bottom left:

MANHATTAN GLASSWARE BY ANCHOR HOCKING. This was the touch of class glass that brought affordable elegance to the tables of millions of American homes. It would have looked right in the most ideal Deco decor, where cost was no object. They also named it right. There's a lot of it around at very reasonable prices. Small side dishes, $5.00. Serving bowls, $12.00 – 18.00. Serving platter, $25.00. With four glass inserts, up to $50.00. Vase, $18.00.

bottom right:

CHASE TIDY CRUMBER AND SILENT BUTLER. Chasing the tidy table was a delight with the Chase tidy crumber set and the Chase silent butler. Both featured buttery Bakelite handles. My stars, they somehow looked and felt just right. Crumber Set, $35.00 – 50.00. Silent Butler, $55.00 – 75.00.

vanity fare

dresser & dresser sets —

When times are tough, a woman can take pleasure in lavishing some extra time on looking ravishing. Without spending lavishly. And the Deco period had much to offer a woman in movie star style at a modest price.

The look and the feel of a woman's private luxuries offer a touch of glamour that frees the spirit from the realities of the everyday.

The vanity itself often set the stage for a fine array of actors in this playful vanity. Often dramatically excessive, the Deco vanity encouraged a woman to engage in dramatic vanity, if only for her own amusement. So join us on a tour of little delights which helped women everywhere realize their fantasies, and gave them respite from the harsh truths of Depression era living.

above left:

FRENCH DUAL POD VANITY. My personal favorite vanity style is this: full-length mirror in the center with pods on either side. This one, made in France, features beautifully fluted side units with swing-out doors. But that's purely a stylistic judgment. My guess is that women prefer a vanity that's more intimate, with plenty of room on the surface for the little treasures that make sprucing up into a relaxed beauty ritual. A not-too-affordable $2,000.00.

above right:

VANITY BY SIMMONS. The Simmons company did a most remarkable thing in the 30s. They introduced a line of steel bedroom furniture in several different styles, designed by Norman Bel Geddes, one of the true geniuses of the Deco era. In this style, the wood grain appliqué, as shown, is most unusual. More often these were painted gloss black with cream yellow drawers. Handles were either orange or black Bakelite with a metal strip for strength. These bedroom pieces are highly acclaimed today, and enjoy great acceptance because of their definitive styling. $600.00 – 800.00.

VANITY BY KITTINGER. This is part of a complete bedroom set, and the most unique piece is not the vanity, but the chest of drawers. But the vanity was designed to dazzle, with its modified pod styling accented by vertical half-rounds across the curved surface of each pod. The mirror is free standing and very dramatic. The colors — two shades of gray, a banana yellow stripe, and silver trim — are soft and subtle. All in all, it's just like in the movies. $600.00 – 800.00.

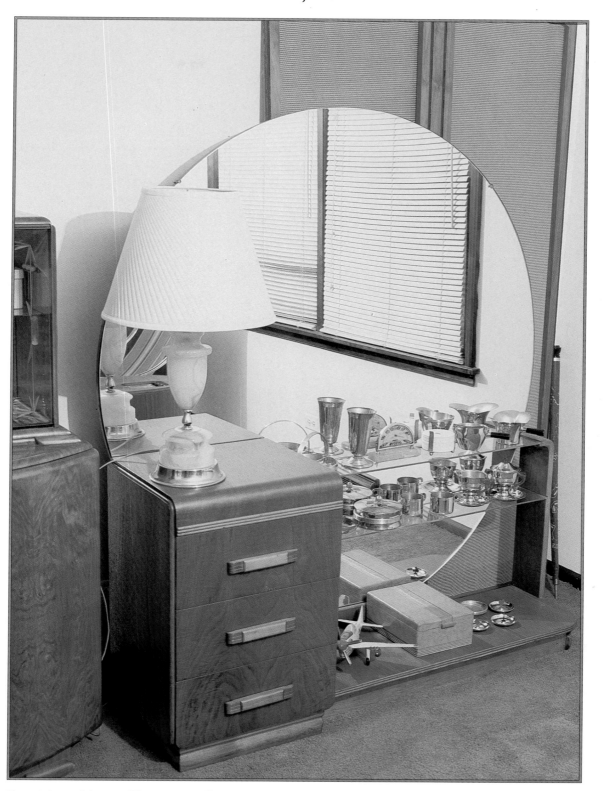

FULL MOON VANITY. This vanity is all mirror. And a huge mirror it is. With glass shelves on the right, providing plenty of room for beauty stuff, and three drawers on the left, it's a lot more practical than it appears at first. The mirror is split, the dividing line concealed by the top shelf. $400.00 – 600.00.

below left:

PAIR OF CIRCLE BASE VANITY LAMPS. The base in black and chrome is handsome enough with its bold circle design. But it's the double-tier helmet shades that make them elegant. We use them with blue bulbs as night lights. They create a sleepy, moody aura. $250.00 – 300.00 the pair.

below right:

FIVE DISC VANITY LAMP. A simple design brought to life by the five cobalt blue glass discs. When the light is turned on, so are the cobalt discs — glittering lightly. $60.00 – 75.00.

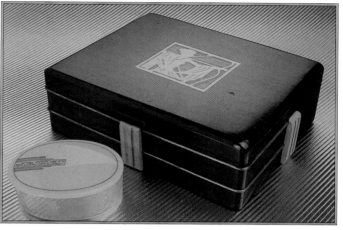

above:

DECO GREEN AND BLACK JEWELRY BOX. Even if the jewelry was inexpensive, this handsome box made it seem valuable. And if it were filled with Bakelite and Catalin jewelry, it would contain a treasure trove of great value today. $45.00 – 75.00.

below:

BRUSH AND MIRROR IN BLACK AND GOLD. Very Deco. Buy only in mint condition. $20.00 – 30.00.

left:

SCULPTURE OF DANCING WOMAN. A spelter sculpture adds a touch of fantasy, and serves as a catch-all. $75.00 – 100.00.

the world's fair

1933 – 1934

Chicago, 1933. The future dawned on America. It was the machine age, the design age, streamline, moderne times. Everything that had been glimpsed in the movies glittered on all sides as the celebration of A Century of Progress opened on the shores of Lake Michigan. It was the most optimistic place in the world.

The Chicago World's Fair promised a new beginning. A new era. A new style of living. A future about to burst forth in glory. And it was so massive in scope, people spent days surrounded by this new kind of opulence. It was a new day inside the fair. And that new day was awesome.

But, alas, outside, the new day never dawned. People went home to their old-fashioned houses and their Depression depression. And the future grew dim in the face of reality. It really never had a chance.

But nearly everybody who shared in the wonder of it all, took home a souvenir or two as gifts for those who had stayed behind. And among them were some truly beautiful things. Collectible reminders of a time which never was. And, oh, what a time it was.

top:

CENTURY OF PROGRESS COMPACTS. They tell the story in black and white. Two very high quality souvenirs presenting the exciting design of the World's Fair logo. Really neat. $40.00 – 65.00.

middle:

THE OFFICIAL COMMEMORATIVE MEDAL. It reflects the dramatic linear sculpture of the time. Robust as Depression art, yet the epitome of classic Art Deco. This one came with its original informative folder and glassine envelope. $60.00 – 90.00.

right:

A CENTURY OF PROGRESS BELT BUCKLE. A handsome piece of work with the Deco design logo. $35.00 – 55.00.

top left:

THE 1933 FORD TAXI. Toys were extremely popular souvenirs, because most out-of-towners left the kids at home. Arcade of Freeport, Illinois, produced these cast-iron Fords. And the 1933 Fords were a styling and performance breakthrough for Ford. It was only six years since Ford was making the rather primitive Model T. $700.00 – 1,000.00+.

top right:

1933 STUDEBAKER LAND CRUISER. It was futuristic to be sure. Skirted fenders. Integrated trunk. Fastback design. And National Products of Chicago made these slush mold cars on an assembly line right there at the fair. So it was educational, too. And it was slightly restyled for 1934 and sold at the fair again. $250.00 – 350.00.

middle & bottom left:

1933 – 1934 WORLD'S FAIR BUSES. General Motors made semi-style buses for the Chicago World's Fair. Like the San Francisco trolleys, the sides were open so one could step on and off at will. Arcade made cast-iron replicas in five sizes from the tiny one-piece model to a large one over a foot long. A size for every budget. They still appear regularly around the Midwest. They sold a bunch of them. From small to large, $160.00, $250.00, $275.00, $400.00, and $850.00 for the large one.

above:

1934 CHRYSLER AIRFLOW. Every so often, one of these appears with the decal just above the rear bumper. At only 4" long, it seems it would have been a popular toy to take home. It would fit nicely in a purse. The 1934 World's Fair season was a short one, and attendance was off. Still it was cheap and a real landmark car much touted at the fair. $200.00+.

1933 PLYMOUTH. Another popular gift, but not as dramatic as the future cars presented there. The ones from the fair have A Century of Progress silk screened on the top. Plain or Dealer imprint, $200.00 – 250.00. World's Fair imprint, $250.00 – 375.00.

right:

COCKTAIL SHAKER. It's covered with drink recipes, the perfect recipe for this moment of repeal. The lid had just come off Prohibition and alcoholic beverages were legal again. The only problem with this souvenir was that the lid wouldn't come off. And when it suddenly let go, friends and family would have all the drinks they chose to wear. Condition varies wildly. $30.00 – 80.00.

top:

POSTCARDS AND DECALS.
Paper souvenirs abounded at the
Chicago World's Fair. A complete collection would be more
than one person could carry alone.
But the most compelling to me are
the postcards which folks attending
sent back home with Wish You
Were Here greetings from the
fair. And pulling into the driveway
upon returning, the decal in the
back window told everyone that
you were among those lucky people who had experienced the wonder of it all first hand. Postcards
around $5.00 each. Decal,
$8.00 – 10.00.

middle left:

THE TOOTHPICK WOOD-
PECKER. These were not exclu-
sively products of the World's
Fair. But the souvenirs are clearly
marked. The bird tilts forward and
picks up a toothpick. Silly?
Absolutely. $20.00 – 50.00.
Not really worth it.

middle right:

STACKING ASHTRAYS. They
were cheap and almost totally use-
less as ashtrays. But they were
cute little souvenirs for Bert and
Mable next door. $5.00 each.

bottom:

CIGARETTE CASE. Quite
attractive and a nice memory of a
wonderful trip into the future.
$20.00 – 40.00.

the desk set

There were some very swank offices in the Deco period. Advertising agencies and radio stations reveled in the avant garde impression machine age/Deco provided. Just like in the movies. Only purer. And the receptionist may have had the most glamourous desk of all. For it was she who made the first and lasting impression.

Meanwhile, in the trenches, the everyday worker at his very ordinary desk and stoic office setting, needed to appear as "with it" as his peers. And there was no shortage of office delights that Deco could bring his way.

And so his desk and walls soon became a fantasy island in a sea of distant past. And his spirits must have been lifted by the hope and optimism of such a sight.

previous page:

ROYAL CHROME DESK. In black wood on a tapered chrome tube framework, this desk is Deco style at its best. It's light, lively, and very avant garde. Attributed to the design talents of the fabulous Donald Deskey. Barely affordable at $600.00 – 900.00.

right:

STRAP DESK BY KOCH COMPANY OF CHICAGO. One of my favorites, this desk is done in black painted wood on an ingenious chrome strap framework. Shelves fit neatly into the curved sections at either end. The top is a black Bakelite-type material. Also less affordable at $700.00 – 900.00.

bottom left:

BAROMETER. Created by Middlebury Electric Clock Company, this barometer practically screams machine age/Art Deco. The instant I saw it I had to have it. $75.00 – 100.00+.

bottom right:

BAROMETER BY TAYLOR. In dark brown and butterscotch Catalin. Very pretty. $35.00 – 45.00.

top:

AUTO DESK CALENDAR BY EGZ. Produced in Germany, this ingenious gadget no longer works right. But it still looks right. $35.00 – 40.00.

middle:

DIPADAY DESK SET. Produced by Sengbusch, this desk set inkwell has style to spare. But who used dip pens in the enlightened age of the 1930s? $40.00.

below:

CATALIN DOUBLE INK WELL DESK PEN CADDY. If looks could kill, this would surely be one killer piece. It's heavy. And it's about as much butterscotch Catalin as I've see in one place. $125.00 – 175.00+.

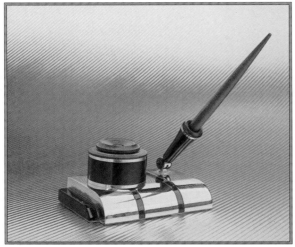

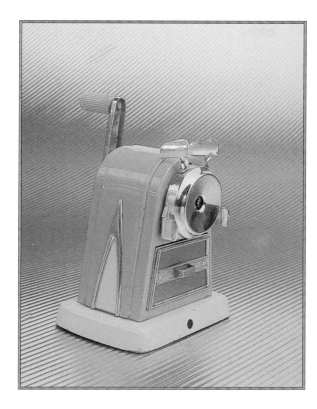

top left:
AQUA AND CREAM PENCIL SHARPENER. $60.00 – 80.00.

top right:
MAROON AND CHROME PENCIL SHARPENER. $35.00 – 50.00.

bottom left:
BROWN AND CHROME FOUNTAIN PEN HOLDER. Very dignified Deco. $15.00 – 20.00.

bottom right:
RED AND CHROME STREAMLINE PEN HOLDER. Deco, Deco, Deco. It's that exciting. $50.00 – 75.00+.

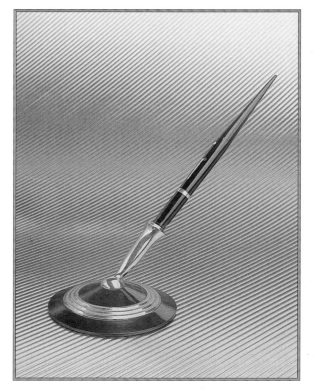

top left:
DESKTOP PICTURE FRAME. The chrome ball holds one side, the cylinder holds the other. It fits the Deco desk like it was made for it. And it probably was. $45.00 – 75.00+.

right:
DESKTOP CHROME AND BAKELITE BY DURA-FRAME. Ours still has Katherine Hepburn in it, just as it came from the store. I've seen these priced as high as $300.00. It's great, but not that great. $125.00 – 150.00.

bottom left:
CHROME SWIVEL PICTURE FRAME. This is a very pretty Deco frame. It just looks right. $50.00 – 65.00.

top right:
MACHINE AGE BOOKENDS. Very masculine. And very much an indication of the powerful hold machine age manufacturing had on the male psyche. Neat. $100.00 – 125.00.

DESK LAMPS

middle right:
MACHINE AGE DESK LAMP. Straight cut gears combine with worm gears to produce an elegant piece of machine age art for the desk. Chrome plated, of course. $175.00 – 250.00.

bottom right:
THE CLASSIC DECO DESK LAMP BY MARKEL. This wonderful lamp combined a conservative directness with many delightful Deco lines. The multi-disc off-on switch tower being the best. $225.00 – 300.00.

below:
CHASE CIRCULAR DESK LAMP. It starts with the simplest of geometric shapes. And flutes the circle with parallel lines. It would look so fine with a metal shade. $75.00 – 125.00.

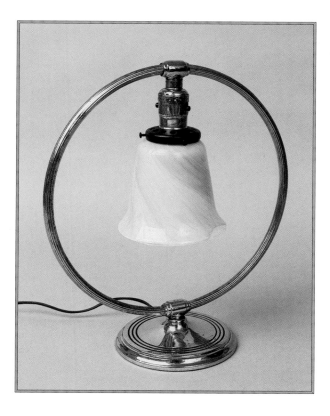

previous page, top left:

MICROPHONE DESK LAMP. With its microphone shape and blue mirrored inset, it reflects the glamour of radio at the time. A very dramatic and unusual lamp. $125.00 – 150.00.

previous page, top right:

BLACK AND SILVER DESK LAMP. The double discs on the stem give this lamp strong Deco identity. $60.00 – 75.00.

previous page, bottom left:

NUDE SUNBATHER DESK LAMP. For fashion or beauty shop, it spelled out beauty in a most direct way. $125.00 – 150.00.

previous page, bottom right:

TRIPLE TIER DESK LAMP. Most appropriate for the lady's writing desk, this lamp is scaled down to size and styled to satisfy the lady's desire for dramatic flair. The three-tier design lets light play out patterns on the surface, while the soft green painted interior of the shade plays a little game with color. $125.00 – 150.00.

DESKTOP CARAFES

right:

DECO GREEN CARAFE. American Thermos Bottle Company designed it in the right Deco color. $40.00 – 60.00.

below:

BREWSTER GREEN MANNING BOWMAN CARAFE WITH TRAY. When it came to designers, Manning Bowman hired or contracted some of the very best. The design and color of this carafe is choice. $70.00 – 125.00.

right:
DECO GREEN
MANNING BOWMAN
CARAFE. Medium-high
style in the right Deco green
with a clear glass stopper.
$50.00 – 60.00.

below:
PINK MANNING BOWMAN CARAFE WITH TRAY.
Women were just beginning to demand and earn positions of
leadership. In advertising, fashion, and cosmetics in particu-
lar. Aware as they were, Manning Bowman fashioned a
carafe and tray for the desk marked "Hers." It's slender,
lighter, and pretty in pink. $45.00 – 65.00.

above:
CHROME MANNING BOWMAN CARAFE.
Again highly designed, but more direct than oth-
ers. $30.00 – 40.00.

left:
ALUMINUM CARAFE BY
KROMEX. The drama is all in
the big aluminum ball on the
top. $20.00 – 25.00.

decoratives

It's a treat for your eyes to accessorize.

Finally, when your house is all Deco-ed, you can begin having fun with the excess wonderful Deco things you just couldn't live without. It's called revolving Deco.

Every now and then when nobody's around you grab all the Deco goodies off all the tables and put them all away. And take out all those wonderful Deco things you haven't seen for a while and put them on all the empty tables. And wait for the ooohs and aaahs.

Well, it may be a long wait. To some people, an all Deco house is such a mind numbing experience, they see everything at once and never focus on one thing. Just can't see the trees for the forest. But think how much you'll enjoy the fun of seeing these almost forgotten treasures all over again.

VASES, CENTERPIECES, AND CANDLESTICKS

top:
CONSOLE SET IN BLACK AND CHROME. Simple lines and Saturn rings let this bowl and candlesticks set make an eloquent Deco statement. Daring in design, but oh so elegant. $150.00 – 175.00.

second from top:
CONSOLE SET IN CHROME AND OLIVE. The olive Bakelite speaks in subdued tones, making this bowl and candlesticks set an enduring companion. It whispers good taste. $125.00 – 150.00.

second from bottom:
Three Conversation Pieces in Red and Chrome. PAIR OF CANDLESTICKS IN CHROME AND CATALIN. The red Catalin circles make the solid Deco statement. $100.00 – 125.00. DOUBLE CANDLE-STICK. Again chrome and Catalin work together to make a delightful piece. $60.00 – 75.00. COMPOTE WITH RED ACCENT BALL. $25.00 – 35.00.

bottom:
CHASE COMPTON CONSOLE BOWL. With its yellowed ivory Bakelite base and unadorned shape, the Compton is striking in its simplicity. They work wonders in pairs. Condition is critical. $60.00 – 110.00.

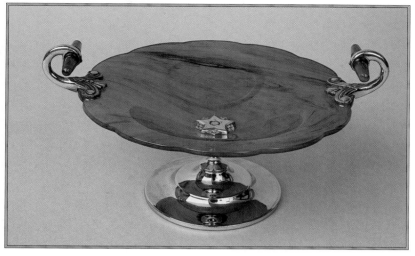

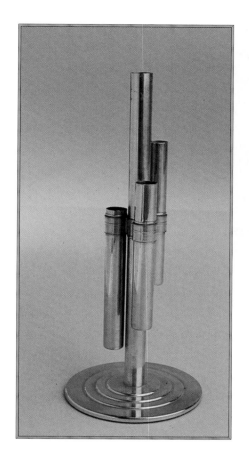

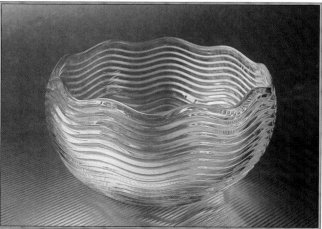

top right:
MANNING BOWMAN CELLULOID CONSOLE BOWL. At least I think it's very heavy celluloid. The chrome handles have matching inserts. In the right light, it glows. $75.00 – 125.00.

top left:
FOUR-TUBE BUD VASE BY CHASE. These are neat. Also, there was a counterfeit, so look for the Chase logo. Chase, $25.00 – 35.00. Counterfeit, $12.00 – 15.00.

middle right:
FARBERWARE BUD VASE. Everyone seems to find this bud vase extremely attractive, overlooking the apparent despair of these stylishly angular ladies. $60.00 – 75.00.

bottom right:
CAST GLASS CENTERPIECE. A sort of modified Manhattan design but quite delightfully wavy. It's large enough to serve punch. And smart enough for wax fruit. $35.00 – 50.00.

top left:
MANHATTAN VASE BY ANCHOR HOCKING. A classic. Very popular. A great value new. So it's a great value today. $18.00.

top middle:
CRYSTAL CUT GLASS VASE. Geometric use of parallel speed lines make this a Deco delight. I must admit, I might be way off on this one. It could be cast glass, though I couldn't find a trace of a casting line. It separates sunlight into spectrum. But I'm guessing on the value. Points for honesty? $150.00 – 250.00.

top right:
LARGE GLASS VASE. Geometric patterns in clear and frosted glass give this vase Deco boldness and beauty. $65.00 – 85.00.

above:
CONSOLE BOWL IN BLACK AND SILVER. Some things just look so right. This is one of them. I'm not even sure it's from the 30s. That's why the low estimate. $35.00 – 50.00.

SCULPTURE

The bronzes in our home are all affordable
reproductions of the work of Chiparis.
Except for the ones shown here. Most of our
old sculpture is plaster and fun.

right:

Right: THE GYMNAST. Plaster. Exquisitely tinted.
It's a bit of a puzzle. $125.00 – 150.00. Left:
DECO-MAN. These were probably store props in a
men's suitery. We use them as a way of poking fun at
some of the excesses of the time. $50.00 – 75.00.

below:

PLASTER OF WOMAN AND GREYHOUND. Really
a wonderful period piece and a great pleasure. You
just don't dare think about it too much, lest it become
rather silly. $225.00 – 300.00.

bottom right:

CHIPARIS-STYLE DANCING WOMAN. Very styl-
ish in bronze with polished highlights and ivory.
$800.00 – 1,000.00.

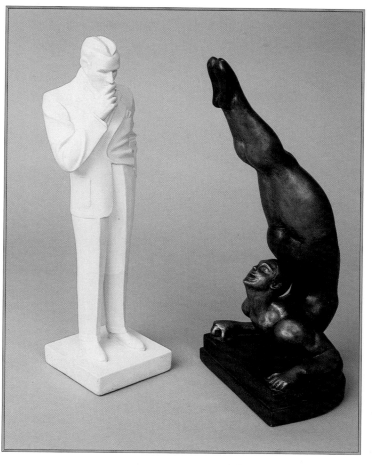

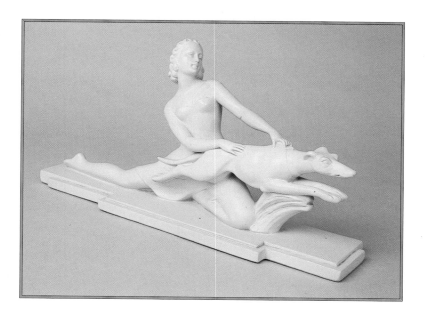

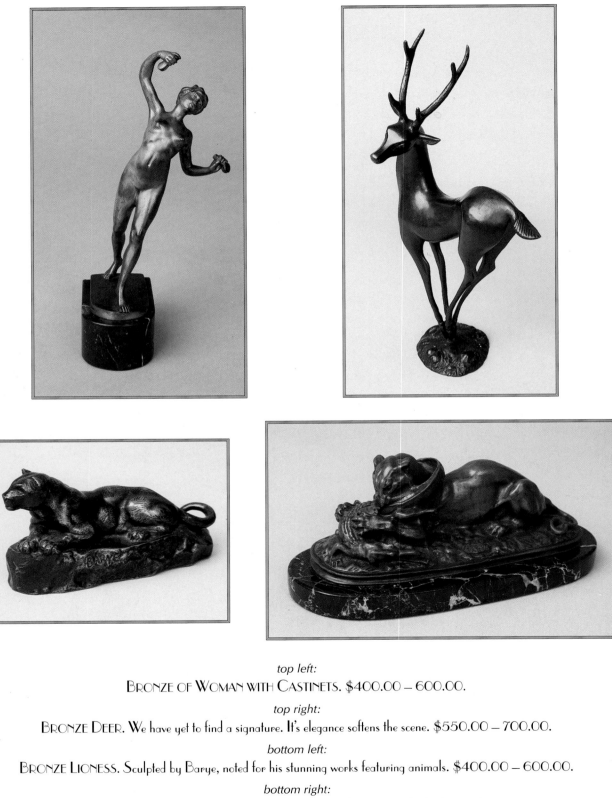

top left:
BRONZE OF WOMAN WITH CASTINETS. $400.00 – 600.00.

top right:
BRONZE DEER. We have yet to find a signature. It's elegance softens the scene. $550.00 – 700.00.

bottom left:
BRONZE LIONESS. Sculpted by Barye, noted for his stunning works featuring animals. $400.00 – 600.00.

bottom right:
BRONZE LION WITH CROCODILE. Again, a Barye sculpture, more dramatic, and a bit larger. $500.00 – 700.00.

CLOCKS

Streamline Deco clocks came in all manner of designs. A great many were within easy reach of most Americans, even in those hard times. Today, these high-fashion windups don't have to work, after all, who has time to wind them. They provide a Deco lift.

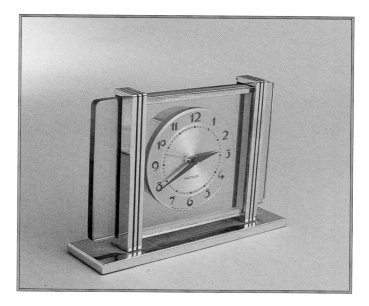

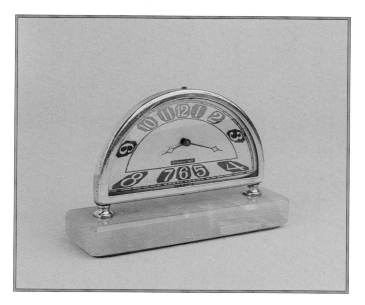

top right:
STREAMLINE CLOCK BY WESTCLOX. This clock design makes one of the purist, simplest, most direct Deco statements a clock could hope to make. Readily available, too. $65.00 – 85.00. If it works, add 20%.

bottom right:
SEMI-ELLIPTIC BY SILVERCRAFT. This was just one of those lucky finds at a flea market. With its marble base and extreme design, it's a wonderful bit of Deco decor. $75.00 – 135.00.

bottom left:
PROMOTIONAL CLOCK FOR GOODYEAR. For the Deco collector. For the automobilia collector. A neat clock. $125.00+.

left:

GENERAL ELECTRIC REFRIGERATOR PROMO-TIONAL CLOCK. This is very well made. And it also enjoys an appeal to several different market segments. Advertising being first in line. $400.00 – 550.00.

bottom center:

DECO INTERPRETATION OF A MANTLE CLOCK. Using tubing and balls to draw the outline of the traditional mantle clock, this clock by Mastercrafters make the traditional go Deco. $125.00 – 150.00.

below:

HEXAGONAL WIND-UP BY WESTCLOX. Nice design. Nice materials. Nice. $25.00 – 30.00.

right:

ORANGE CATALIN WIND-UP BY NUART. The picture says all that needs to be said. $35.00 – 50.00.

bottom right:

WIND-UP EIGHT-DAY CLOCK. This is a remarkably fine design. Deco definitive. $65.00 – 85.00 in working order.

below:

MOOD LAMP, A BALL ON A PEDESTAL. Very Deco base holding a dramatic Saturn ball. Keep this light down low. $100.00 – 135.00.

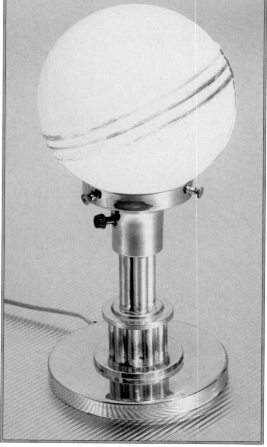

doing it all deco

One reason Art Deco furniture is so hard to find is that back in the 1930s, streamline furnishings were so impossible to blend in with the furniture a couple bought when they set up housekeeping. Deco demanded commitment. And in this all or nothing at all environment, most people had to settle for nothing at all. Except for the radio, the refrigerator, and other appliances that were virtually new to the market so, of course, their manufacturers made them look new.

Today, Deco mixes well with many contemporary styles, but only up to a point. And that's the point at which Deco becomes everything!

Thereafter, when a Deco piece comes in, an old familiar piece of furniture must go out. To a garage sale, an auction, an antique dealer, your just-starting-out kids, or — sigh — off to Goodwill.

For some people, collecting Deco is an invigorating new enthusiasm that gets them out of the house and off exploring antique malls, Sunday flea markets, and auctions. And the delight of finding just the right piece at just the right price (or a little more) is energizing and incredibly refreshing. This project of re-creation is the best kind of recreation.

LIVING ROOM

GILBERT ROHDE RECLINING CHAIR AND
OTTOMAN. Produced around 1935 by Troy Sun-
shade Company, this Gilbert Rohde design is
among my personal favorites. It's beautiful from every
angle. Especially from ¾ rear, where the frame tubes
sweep up and forward to form the arms. This is one
piece that lured me far beyond my arbitrary price
limit. $2,000.00 – 2,500.00.

STREAMLINE CHAIRS. We see the couch version fairly often around the Midwest. It may be a safe bet to attribute the design to Lloyd. The couches are too long, giving them the appearance of waiting benches. But chairs are slim and delightfully "speedy." They are crisp and clean. Needing cushions redone, $350.00 each. With excellent original or redone cushions, $600.00 each. TWO-PLACE ULTRA DECO COUCH. If there is a design for upholstered furniture that screams streamline Deco, this is it. Produced by Royalchrome, sometimes attributed to Donald Deskey, these pieces capture the joy and confidence in future like nothing else. They are outrageous — and yet, after living with this design, it settles comfortably in. What at first seems almost like whimsical caricature, later seems an artistic expression of optimism. A wonderful design. Re-issued today. Ours is an original and rather tacky. Originals are very hard to find. $1,200.00 – 3,500.00+. SMALL SET OF FIREPLACE TOOLS. Seen in the background, these tools and rack are a neat addition to any Deco fireplace setting. All chrome with yellow Bakelite knobs. $125.00 – 150.00. STORE DISPLAY SHELF UNITS. We chose not to use them as shelving, but rather as decorative art on either side of our fireplace. The panels were salvaged from the old Mercury Theater in Chicago. Deco dealers and collectors really need shelving units, and that drives the price up. The price listed here is exactly what we had to pay for them. They sure do add a dramatic flair to the fireplace wall, though. $350.00. You may have to pay substantially more.

right:

SLING CHAIR AND OTTOMAN BY MCKAY. Produced by McKay, designed by Beveloqua, these chairs are sought by collectors. This one features a wide spring steel chrome band. Strangely, the ottoman may be worth more than the chair. The fabric sling is incredibly easy to replace. Chair, $450.00 – 500.00. Ottoman, $350.00 – 450.00. If rechroming is required, subtract $100.00.

bottom right:

SLING CHAIRS BY MCKAY. Legend has it that these chairs were featured in the Florida exhibit at the Chicago World's Fair. The most popular McKays, these high back slings feature slender spring steel chrome bands. $650.00 – 750.00 each. If rechroming is required, subtract $100.00.

below:

BARCELONA CHAIR BY MIES VAN DER ROHE. Designed for a 1929 exhibit, these chairs, couches, and ottomans continue to bring top dollar. They have been produced and copied ever since, by licensed and unlicensed manufacturers. Therefore, the prices are all over the place. Perhaps the best values are those without the pedigree. Oh, the cat is Tigger the Ocicat. He has a pedigree. $300.00 – 1,500.00+.

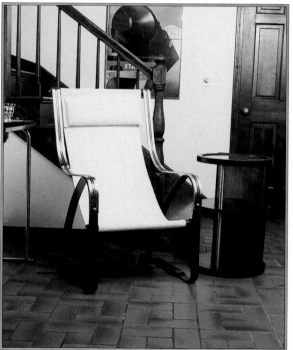

top left:

SNAIL CHAIRS. Where's Jean Harlow when you need her. These chairs have a kind of Deco decadence. They're fun and kind of funny. And very suggestive. We keep a mannequin lounging in one. $250.00 – 300.00 each.

bottom left:

GRAND CONFORT TWO-PLACE COUCH. Designed by Le Corbusier in 1928, the Grand Confort furniture created a very simple concept by constructing a graceful steel tube frame, chrome plated, and stuffing cushions on either end, in back and bottom. And it works. The back and seat cushions hold the end cushions firmly in place. And the slight wraparound of the front of the frame, holds them back. Very comfortable. And one of the most glamorous designs of all time. The design continues to be produced, although they are quite pricey. In leather they bring more than in fabric. I've seen a wide range of prices. $1,200.00 – 2,500.00. FRENCH PILLAR COFFEE TABLE. With its fluted base, it is a very formal sort of Deco. Very handsome. $250.00 – 300.00. SCULPTURE OR BOWL STANDS. The long, wide chrome over steel "U" straps create real magic with these lovely tables. If you're looking for a place to put your "jazz bowl," and don't have a large dog, one of these would do the trick. Very glamourous. $750.00 – 1,000.00 each. A PAIR OF SCONCES. I saw these a long time back, and spent years hoping to find a pair. They're round and chrome with a center hook that holds two circles of frosted glass. These appeared in an auction catalog, and I went just to buy them, no matter what. Later my friend sold his pair for more. But this is what we paid. $800.00+.

right:

COPPER-PLATED CURVED STRAP CONSOLE TABLE. Fine dark veneers and black trim serve as the frame for the delightful long curved copper-plated steel straps and parallel support straps that tie it all together. It is definitive streamline Deco. Yet so elegant. $2,500.00 – 3,500.00.

bottom left:

STEP END TABLES. Designed by Alphonse Bach. Produced by Lloyd. These triple tube tables are highly sought after. Generally purchased in pairs for either end of the couch, they have an upper lamp level and a lower stuff level. Even today, most people will not buy just one. $300.00 each. $800.00+ for the pair.

bottom right:

ROUND SIDE TABLE BY HOWELL. The curved strap legs give this table a special panache. The top is a black Bakelite sort of material. It was probably the work of Wolfgang Hoffman. $300.00 – 400.00.

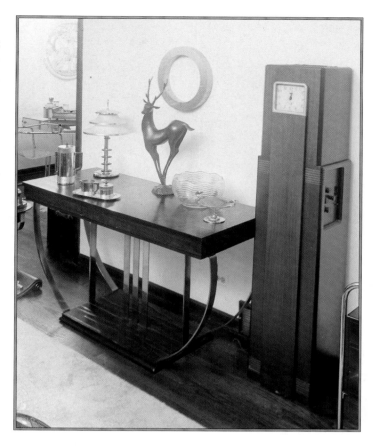

left:

WOLFGANG HOFFMAN SMALL ROUND TABLE. These were and are real winners. Produced by the Howell Company of Geneva, Illinois, the three-tube leg design, high quality chrome plating, and the contrasting high gloss Bakelite-like black tops give these tables Deco bona fides. Most often sold in pairs. $250.00 – 300.00 each.

bottom left:

WOLFGANG HOFFMAN FOYER TABLE. I saw one of these at a modernism show with an asking price of $3,500.00. Really, now. These are wonderful tables, allowing a guest one last look at themselves, and to leave their card on a tray, before they enter the fray. Gee, I can't even get guests to knock the snow off their shoes. Produced by Howell, these handsome tables always do well at twentieth century auctions. And rightly so. $1,400.00 – 1,700.00.
DOUBLE-TIER SIDE TABLE. Round, with an enclosed backside, this walnut and black table features a top with a mirrored strip around the outer edge and a single plated rod in the center front. Very pretty, it softens a room. $400.00 – 500.00.

bottom right:

MULTI-LEG ENTRY TABLE. The maker is unidentified. But these eight-legged tables were just the place for the silver Deco tray on which the butler could place a guest's calling card. Oh, my. Well, we don't use ours that way, but used any old way, you'll enjoy its classic Deco elegance. $800.00 – 900.00.

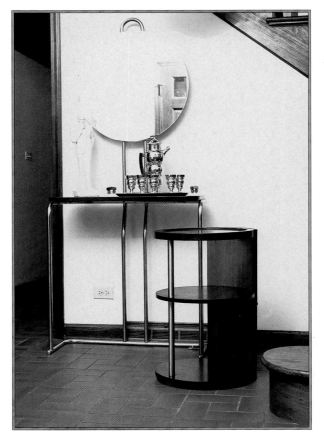

right:

REVERSE TORCHIERE LAMP. Designed by Walter von Nessen, it features the popular multi-disc idiom. But it's the shade that creates the drama. It literally turns the segmented torchiere bell upside down. So doing, the light plays dramatically with the table top, while the bells broadcast a gentle glow. This is one sweet lamp. $400.00 – 500.00.

below:

FROSTED GLASS LAMP. This is a most remarkable lamp. It's large. And very heavy. After all, it has no fewer than 20 frosted glass panels in the base, and another four panels in the polished stainless steel shade. The framework is also constructed of stainless steel. We use a blue bulb in the base, just to create a mood. The upper light is just a frosted 100 watt bulb. Of course, both bottom and top lights can be operated independently. So far we have not been able to attribute this design. But the designer was a talent, no question about that. $800.00 – 1,000.00+. *Note: The sculpture is *Two Thoroughbreds*. A ferrari by Stanley Wanlass.

TABLE LAMPS

I've never liked table lamps much. They always seems sort of phony. So contrived, trying to look like something else. A fancy vase or sculpture or whatever, with a light socket plopped on top.

But machine age Deco lamps are different. They were conceived and designed to be lamps. Period. And to me, that's the way a lamp ought to be.

left:

ART GLASS TABLE LAMP. They came in with the Deco period. And when it ended, they were gone. Yet they were bright refreshments by day, and cozy companions by night. The light in the base makes a perfect night light. Turn the switch and it switches to the regular reading lamp on top. Switch it again, and you can enjoy both. And if the night light is too bright, just change to a darker color Christmas tree bulb. $100.00 – 150.00.

below:

KID'S ROOM AIRPLANE NIGHT LIGHT. It's a novelty light of the period. It glows blue at night. And it's fun. $150.00 – 200.00.

*Note: also see vanity lamps and desk lamps in those sections.

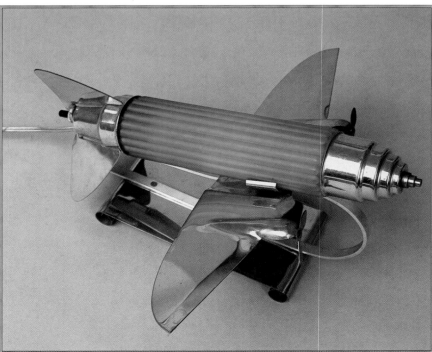

RADIOS

right:

CHAIRSIDE RADIO BY WESTINGHOUSE. Most people call it the Empire State radio, because of its skyscraper design. It is properly called the Column Air. The speaker is on the top, controls on the side at chair height. A fabulous design. Very heavy. $350.00 – 600.00.

below:

CHAIRSIDE RADIO BY PHILCO. A pretty oval design, but with only three legs, prone to falling over. It has a nice table surface, but anything wet will ruin the veneer. $225.00 – 300.00.

bottom:

CHAIRSIDE RADIO BY ZENITH. What a spectacular design. It picks up the surround louvres of the fabulous 810 Cord automobile. Powerful — with all the tricks built in. One cannot help but imagine the king of the castle in his streamline leather chair listening to the war news on short wave in the early 40s. Very masculine. Very Deco. Very expensive then — very expensive now. $800.00 – 1,200.00.

OVERHEAD LIGHTING

There are some very neat overhead fixtures. But they're few and far between. Each fixture shown here was purchased without a moment's hesitation. A terrific ceiling or wall fixture is so desirable, you often don't have the luxury of thinking twice.

top left:
COBALT BLUE GLASS CHANDELIER. An elegant design featuring 10 cobalt blue discs. One below each light, and five running up the center stalk. Late 30s — early 40s. $375.00 – 500.00.

left:
FLOATING CUSTARD GLASS AND MIRRORED SAUCER. I guess all our overheads are on rheostats. When this one is turned way down, it just hovers in space. Very heavy custard glass section. $300.00 – 450.00.

above:
FORMAL DECO GLOBE AND DECORATIVE BASE. $200.00 – 275.00.

OTHER HOME FURNISHINGS

right:

GRANDFATHER-SIZE CLOCK. We found this in a shop in Wilmette, Illinois. It is quite large. The side panels and lower center panels feature lights behind frosted glass. The center is also lighted from either side, as if a special display area was intended. It was probably used in a commercial application, but that's just a guess. It is spectacular. Not too affordable. $1,500.00 – 2,000.00.

below:

BIRD CAGE AND STAND. Just the place to stuff a parrot. There are a lot of bird cages around, but it pays to look for the best design. We found this dramatic stand, with its long chrome accents, by accident. And tried several nice cages in it, but none of them looked right. Finally we found this round cage by Hendryx. It works. Combined, they have the look. And you don't need the bother of some nasty old bird to enjoy it. Cage, $100.00 – 150.00. Stand, $125.00 – 175.00.

left:

ANDIRONS. When we re-did the fireplace, using ceramic on steel panels from the old Mercury Theatre in Chicago, we put andirons on our mental list. We did find a couple pairs in the $500.00+ range which were Deco enough. When we found this set, plus one spare unit, for $130.00, we were ecstatic. But the fact remains: a Deco set of andirons can be pricey. But they make a bold statement in a Deco fireplace. $350.00 – 450.00.

below right:

ROUND DECO CHINA CABINETS. These circular or modified circular cabinets do appear from time to time, often marked not for sale by the antique dealer who has one. Usually, they can be persuaded to sell, if they can see a profit and enough to pay for a different display and get it free. It isn't easy. And if it's a Deco dealer, forget it. Or trade something very special for it. All about the same, $350.00 – 550.00.

below left:

WALLHANGING OF DIANA AND HOUND. It's made of steel and gesso. Neat. $350.00 – 450.00.

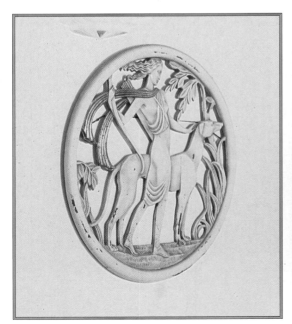

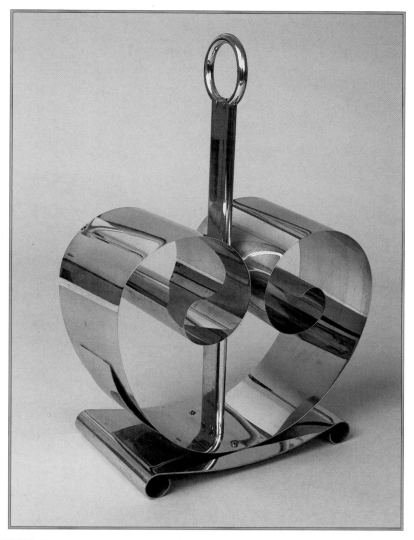

right:

MAGAZINE RACK. Norman Bel Geddes designed it. Revere produced it. Great style. It came different ways. Some have a black Bakelite loop at the top and plugs in the ends of the tube feet. Either way, a stunning accessory. $125.00 – 160.00.

below:

WASTEBASKETS. Wastebaskets don't seem to have been a Deco period priority. But here's a pair. They're also elegant planters for artificial trees. $40.00 – 60.00.

BEDROOM DRESSER BY KITTINGER. One of the most unique chests we've ever seen. Classically elegant. The center line of drawers is rather shallow. But it features a complete set of drawers on either end which are deep. This holds a ton of stuff. And it sets a dramatic tone. The colors are wonderful. $1,000.00+. The complete set: Twin beds, night stand, chest, and vanity with mirror: $2,500.00+.

NOTE: For additional bedroom furnishings, including the Kittinger vanity, see the Vanity Fare Section.

SOMEONE'S IN THE KITCHEN WITH DECO

STREAMLINED STOVE BY NEW PERFECTION. There's a big name designer behind this. It has style. This one uses kerosene, so we don't use it. It's just decoration. But it sets a special scene for the kitchen. $600.00 to $1,000.00 in perfect condition. POTS AND PANS BY KOOK KING. Deco style and colors, and inside some, measures running up the side. $25.00 – 30.00 each. If you see a set, buy it.

TABLE TOP OVEN BY EUREKA. Even at Eureka, they must have shouted *eureka* when they came up with this one. What a concept. The main body is a toaster oven. But, with the release of a lever on either side, hot plates swing out and *voila* — or should I have shouted *eureka!* — put on the coffee. $125.00 – 165.00. Note: Both this and the stove were found in fashionable Door County, Wisconsin. They were in a very elaborate summer home. The stove was in the outdoor cookhouse. The oven in the kitchen. They were perfect.

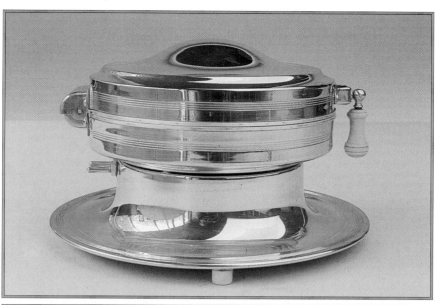

top:
WAFFLE IRON BY UNIVERSAL.
Their slogan, "the name that's
known in every home." Like many
waffle irons, very Deco. Most show
up with little or no use. $25.00.

middle:
WAFFLE IRON BY SAMPSON.
What a handsome Deco design.
Even when not in use, leave it out.
$30.00 – 40.00.

bottom:
WAFFLE IRON BY GENERAL
ELECTRIC. $25.00.

left:
KITCHEN SCALE. Universal made it. The weight is displayed on a rotary dial at the base of the front. It handles up to 24 pounds. Neat design and good color. You can make good buys on these. $15.00 – 30.00.

below:
GENERAL ELECTRIC KITCHEN SUGAR AND CREAMER. Very nicely styled, this set with black trim and red accents was designed to be durable. Everyday as it could be. $30.00 – 40.00.

everything's coming up deco

During the 1930s, everyone producing anything had to have stream-line in mind. Even the most mundane things, with designs that had passed the test of time and remained successful, were redesigned for fear someone else would beat them to it.

That's what this section is about. The ordinary. The everyday. The traditional. The acceptable way things looked. And what they became in the new machine age.

After all, why change an electric fan, a Thermos jug, a fishing reel. Really! And what happened to the vacuum cleaner? Just because it looks faster...does that make it clean any faster?

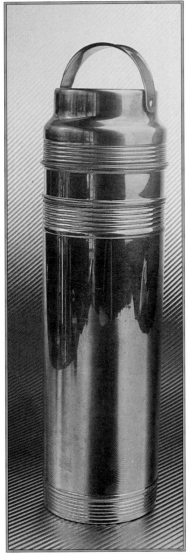

above:
ELECTROLUX VACUUM CLEANER. Designed by
Lurelle Guild for Electrolux and placed on the market in
1937, it looks as if it was designed for speed. Speed lines
and polished aluminum make this humble household
helper an icon of the streamline movement. As a collector, what do you do with it. We have a shelved wall area
on the lower level devoted to design. That seems to work
out well, and attracts a good deal of interest. Now, about
value. This kind of thing is either junk or jewelry,
depending on your point of view. There's one in the
Brooklyn Museum. We found ours, complete, under the
table at a flea market for $5.00. So in this case, the
price is meaningless. But here it is. $15.00 – 150.00.

left:
PICNIC THERMOS BY AMERICAN THERMOS BOT-
TLE COMPANY. A simple cylinder with a handle. Very
machine age appearance. $35.00 – 45.00.

PICNIC JUG THERMOS. Polished aluminum
with black enamel trim. A lot of iced tea in
style. $25.00 – 40.00.

left:

SILVER SWAN OSCILLATING FAN. The entire center section — all in polished aluminum — makes a strong machine age statement. The base is Bakelite. It's Deco delightful. $50.00 – 85.00. At a twentieth century show, much higher.

right:

PURE BREEZE ELECTRIC FAN. The base with its flying buttress support provides Deco interest. Add the two-blade airplane type propeller, and it's a handsome machine age ornament. Manufactured by All-American Mfg. Co. $60.00 – 100.00.

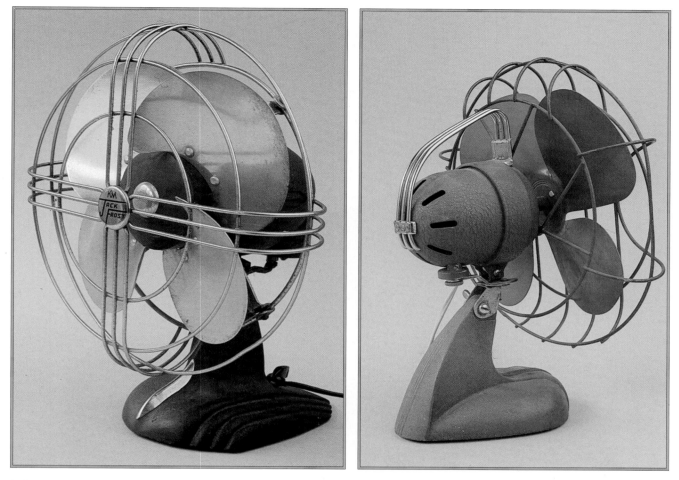

left:

JACK FROST OSCILLATING FAN. Chrome speed lines are the bottom line on this one. $25.00 – 35.00.

right:

HANDY BREEZE OSCILLATING FAN. Chicago Electric Mfg. Co. made this smallish fan. Perhaps as a desk top fan. But to help the buyer find the right niche, they put decorative speed lines to imaginative use as a take-it-along handle. $30.00 – 40.00.

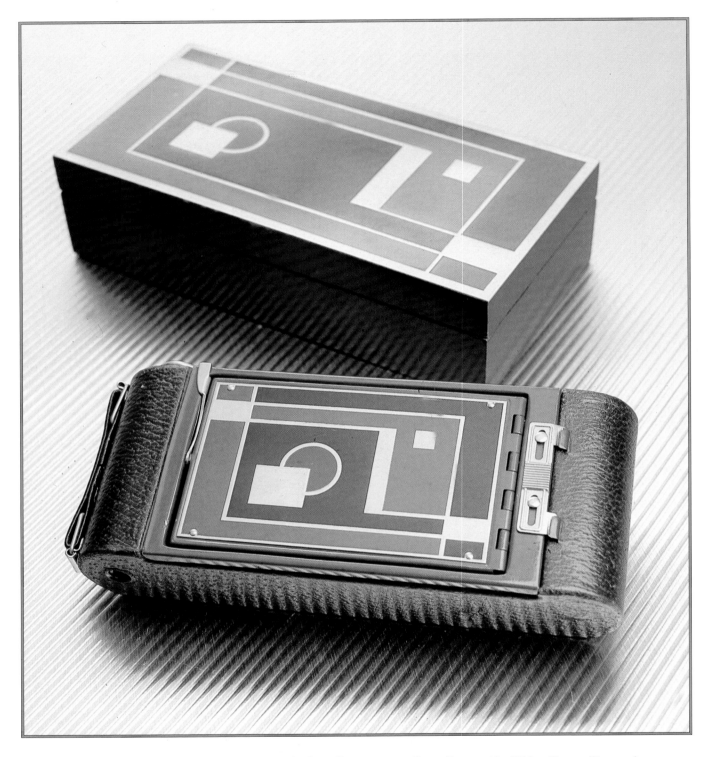

KODAK 1A GIFT CAMERA AND BOX. Designed by Walter Dorwin Teague, this camera has been welcomed to the pantheon of Deco design. The metal plate on the lid of the box makes the box itself a wonderful collectible piece. The design on the camera makes the complete set especially valuable. $600.00 – 900.00. Box alone, $100.00 – 150.00.

top:
KODAK BEAU BROWNIE CAMERA. Less
spectacular, but still impressive, is the design
of the Beau Brownie box camera.
$125.00 – 150.00.

bottom:
KODAK BANTAM SPECIAL CAMERA.
Another great design by Walter Dorwin
Teague, this compact camera has the heft of
real quality. And a delightful look in gloss
black with chrome horizontal parallel lines.
$175.00 – 250.00.

top:

EVEREADY MASTER TABLE LIGHT AND FLASHLIGHT. Very innovative. On the table, just pull up the frosted ball, and the ball glows. But the bottom is a full-fledged flashlight. Just carry it by the ball and point. Very Deco styling. I had one as a kid, and looked a long time to replace it. $50.00 – 75.00.

bottom:

HURD SUPERCASTER. Imagine a fishing reel that looks like this. It came out in the late 1930s. And it had more than looks. Push the button, and internal expansion brakes stopped the reel cold. If your depth perception was good, the line never backlashed. The brake also helped slow the running fish without burning your thumb. I bought one of these during the war with my paper route money. It was $45.00. Mine had been in the store for a long time, so I got it for $27.50. Created by the Hurd Lock Company of Chicago, it was pure machine age design. $100.00 – 125.00.

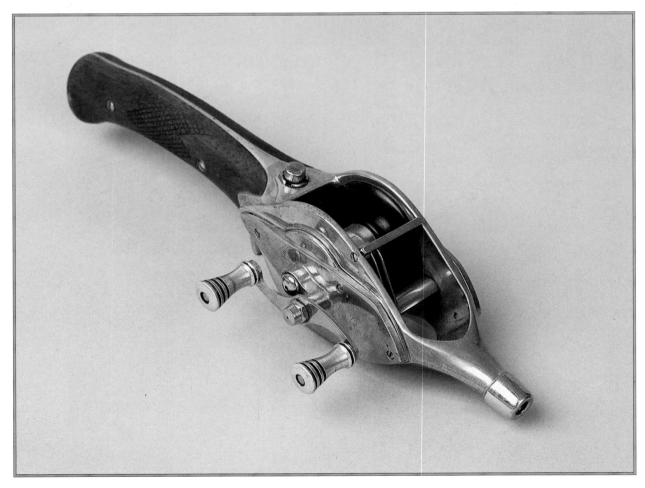

the author & photographer

Author Ken Hutchison

Photographer Greg Johnson with wife Meredith

COLLECTOR BOOKS

Informing Today's Collector

For over two decades we have been keeping collectors informed on trends and values in all fields of antiques and collectibles.

DOLLS, FIGURES & TEDDY BEARS

4707	A Decade of **Barbie** Dolls & Collectibles, 1981–1991, Summers	$19.95
4631	**Barbie** Doll Boom, 1986–1995, Augustyniak	$18.95
2079	**Barbie** Doll Fashion, Volume I, Eames	$24.95
4846	**Barbie** Doll Fashion, Volume II, Eames	$24.95
3957	**Barbie** Exclusives, Rana	$18.95
4632	**Barbie** Exclusives, Book II, Rana	$18.95
4557	**Barbie**, The First 30 Years, Deutsch	$24.95
4847	**Barbie** Years, 1959–1995, 2nd Ed., Olds	$17.95
3310	**Black Dolls**, 1820–1991, Perkins	$17.95
3873	**Black Dolls**, Book II, Perkins	$17.95
3810	**Chatty Cathy Dolls**, Lewis	$15.95
1529	Collector's Encyclopedia of **Barbie** Dolls, DeWein	$19.95
4882	Collector's Encyclopedia of **Barbie** Doll Exclusives and More, Augustyniak	$19.95
2211	Collector's Encyclopedia of **Madame Alexander Dolls**, Smith	$24.95
4863	Collector's Encyclopedia of **Vogue Dolls**, Izen/Stover	$29.95
3967	Collector's Guide to **Trolls**, Peterson	$19.95
4571	**Liddle Kiddles**, Identification & Value Guide, Langford	$18.95
3826	Story of **Barbie**, Westenhouser	$19.95
1513	**Teddy Bears & Steiff** Animals, Mandel	$9.95
1817	**Teddy Bears & Steiff** Animals, 2nd Series, Mandel	$19.95
2084	**Teddy Bears, Annalee's & Steiff** Animals, 3rd Series, Mandel	$19.95
1808	Wonder of **Barbie**, Manos	$9.95
1430	World of **Barbie** Dolls, Manos	$9.95
4880	World of **Raggedy Ann** Collectibles, Avery	$24.95

TOYS, MARBLES & CHRISTMAS COLLECTIBLES

3427	**Advertising Character** Collectibles, Dotz	$17.95
2333	Antique & Collector's **Marbles**, 3rd Ed., Grist	$9.95
3827	Antique & Collector's **Toys**, 1870–1950, Longest	$24.95
3956	Baby Boomer **Games**, Identification & Value Guide, Polizzi	$24.95
4934	**Breyer Animal** Collector's Guide, Identification and Values, Browell	$19.95
3717	**Christmas** Collectibles, 2nd Edition, Whitmyer	$24.95
4976	**Christmas** Ornaments, Lights & Decorations, Johnson	$24.95
4737	**Christmas** Ornaments, Lights & Decorations, Vol. II, Johnson	$24.95
4739	**Christmas** Ornaments, Lights & Decorations, Vol. III, Johnson	$24.95
4649	Classic Plastic **Model Kits**, Polizzi	$24.95
4559	Collectible **Action Figures**, 2nd Ed., Manos	$17.95
3874	Collectible Coca-Cola Toy **Trucks**, deCourtivron	$24.95
2338	Collector's Encyclopedia of **Disneyana**, Longest, Stern	$24.95
4958	Collector's Guide to **Battery Toys**, Hultzman	$19.95
4639	Collector's Guide to **Diecast Toys & Scale Models**, Johnson	$19.95
4651	Collector's Guide to **Tinker Toys**, Strange	$18.95
4566	Collector's Guide to **Tootsietoys**, 2nd Ed., Richter	$19.95
4720	The Golden Age of **Automotive Toys**, 1925–1941, Hutchison/Johnson	$24.95
3436	Grist's Big Book of **Marbles**	$19.95
3970	Grist's Machine-Made & Contemporary **Marbles**, 2nd Ed.	$9.95
4723	**Matchbox** Toys, 1947 to 1996, 2nd Ed., Johnson	$18.95
4871	**McDonald's** Collectibles, Henriques/DuVall	$19.95
1540	**Modern Toys** 1930–1980, Baker	$19.95
3888	**Motorcycle** Toys, Antique & Contemporary, Gentry/Downs	$18.95
4953	Schroeder's Collectible **Toys**, Antique to Modern Price Guide, 4th Ed.	$17.95
1886	Stern's Guide to **Disney** Collectibles	$14.95
2139	Stern's Guide to **Disney** Collectibles, 2nd Series	$14.95
3975	Stern's Guide to **Disney** Collectibles, 3rd Series	$18.95
2028	**Toys**, Antique & Collectible, Longest	$14.95
3979	**Zany Characters** of the Ad World, Lamphier	$16.95

FURNITURE

1457	American **Oak** Furniture, McNerney	$9.95
3716	American **Oak** Furniture, Book II, McNerney	$12.95
1118	Antique **Oak** Furniture, Hill	$7.95
2271	Collector's Encyclopedia of **American** Furniture, Vol. II, Swedberg	$24.95
3720	Collector's Encyclopedia of **American** Furniture, Vol. III, Swedberg	$24.95
3878	Collector's Guide to **Oak** Furniture, George	$12.95
1755	Furniture of the **Depression Era**, Swedberg	$19.95
3906	**Heywood-Wakefield** Modern Furniture, Rouland	$18.95
1885	**Victorian** Furniture, Our American Heritage, McNerney	$9.95
3829	**Victorian** Furniture, Our American Heritage, Book II, McNerney	$9.95

JEWELRY, HATPINS, WATCHES & PURSES

1712	Antique & Collector's **Thimbles** & Accessories, Mathis	$19.95
1748	Antique **Purses**, Revised Second Ed., Holiner	$19.95
1278	Art Nouveau & Art Deco **Jewelry**, Baker	$9.95
4850	Collectible **Costume Jewelry**, Simonds	$24.95
3875	Collecting Antique **Stickpins**, Kerins	$16.95
3722	Collector's Ency. of **Compacts, Carryalls & Face Powder Boxes**, Mueller	$24.95
4854	Collector's Ency. of **Compacts, Carryalls & Face Powder Boxes**, Vol. II	$24.95
4940	**Costume Jewelry**, A Practical Handbook & Value Guide, Rezazadeh	$24.95
1716	Fifty Years of Collectible **Fashion Jewelry**, 1925–1975, Baker	$19.95
1424	**Hatpins** & Hatpin Holders, Baker	$9.95
4570	Ladies' **Compacts**, Gerson	$24.95
1181	100 Years of Collectible **Jewelry**, 1850–1950, Baker	$9.95
4729	**Sewing Tools** & Trinkets, Thompson	$24.95
2348	20th Century Fashionable Plastic **Jewelry**, Baker	$19.95
4878	Vintage & Contemporary **Purse Accessories**, Gerson	$24.95
3830	Vintage **Vanity Bags & Purses**, Gerson	$24.95

INDIANS, GUNS, KNIVES, TOOLS, PRIMITIVES

1868	Antique **Tools**, Our American Heritage, McNerney	$9.95
1426	**Arrowheads** & Projectile Points, Hothem	$7.95
4943	Field Guide to **Flint Arrowheads & Knives** of the North American Indian	$9.95
2279	**Indian Artifacts** of the Midwest, Hothem	$14.95
3885	**Indian Artifacts** of the Midwest, Book II, Hothem	$16.95
4870	**Indian Artifacts** of the Midwest, Book III, Hothem	$18.95
1964	**Indian Axes** & Related Stone Artifacts, Hothem	$14.95
2023	**Keen Kutter** Collectibles, Heuring	$14.95
4724	Modern **Guns**, Identification & Values, 11th Ed., Quertermous	$12.95
2164	**Primitives**, Our American Heritage, McNerney	$9.95
1759	**Primitives**, Our American Heritage, 2nd Series, McNerney	$14.95
4730	Standard **Knife** Collector's Guide, 3rd Ed., Ritchie & Stewart	$12.95

PAPER COLLECTIBLES & BOOKS

4633	**Big Little Books**, Jacobs	$18.95
4710	Collector's Guide to **Children's Books**, Jones	$18.95
1441	Collector's Guide to **Post Cards**, Wood	$9.95
2081	Guide to Collecting **Cookbooks**, Allen	$14.95
2080	Price Guide to **Cookbooks & Recipe Leaflets**, Dickinson	$9.95
3973	**Sheet Music** Reference & Price Guide, 2nd Ed., Pafik & Guiheen	$19.95
4654	**Victorian Trade Cards**, Historical Reference & Value Guide, Cheadle	$19.95
4733	**Whitman Juvenile Books**, Brown	$17.95

GLASSWARE

4561	Collectible **Drinking Glasses**, Chase & Kelly	$17.95
4642	Collectible **Glass Shoes**, Wheatley	$19.95
4937	Coll. **Glassware** from the 40s, 50s & 60s, 4th Ed., Florence	$19.95
1810	Collector's Encyclopedia of **American Art Glass**, Shuman	$29.95
4938	Collector's Encyclopedia of **Depression Glass**, 13th Ed., Florence	$19.95
1961	Collector's Encyclopedia of **Fry Glassware**, Fry Glass Society	$24.95
1664	Collector's Encyclopedia of **Heisey Glass**, 1925–1938, Bredehoft	$24.95
3905	Collector's Encyclopedia of **Milk Glass**, Newbound	$24.95
4936	Collector's Guide to **Candy Containers**, Dezso/Poirier	$19.95
4564	**Crackle Glass**, Weitman	$19.95
4941	**Crackle Glass**, Book II, Weitman	$19.95
2275	**Czechoslovakian Glass** and Collectibles, Barta/Rose	$16.95
4714	**Czechoslovakian Glass** and Collectibles, Book II, Barta/Rose	$16.95
4716	**Elegant Glassware** of the Depression Era, 7th Ed., Florence	$19.95
1380	Encylopedia of **Pattern Glass**, McClain	$12.95
3981	Ever's Standard **Cut Glass** Value Guide	$12.95
4659	**Fenton** Art Glass, 1907–1939, Whitmyer	$24.95
3725	**Fostoria**, Pressed, Blown & Hand Molded Shapes, Kerr	$24.95
4719	**Fostoria**, Etched, Carved & Cut Designs, Vol. II, Kerr	$24.95
3883	**Fostoria Stemware**, The Crystal for America, Long & Seate	$24.95
4644	**Imperial Carnival Glass**, Burns	$18.95

COLLECTOR BOOKS
Informing Today's Collector

3886	**Kitchen Glassware** of the Depression Years, 5th Ed., Florence	$19.95
4725	Pocket Guide to **Depression Glass**, 10th Ed., Florence	$9.95
5035	Standard Encyclopedia of **Carnival Glass**, 6th Ed., Edwards/Carwile	$24.95
5036	Standard **Carnival Glass** Price Guide, 11th Ed., Edwards/Carwile	$9.95
4875	Standard Encyclopedia of **Opalescent Glass**, 2nd ed., Edwards	$19.95
4731	**Stemware Identification**, Featuring Cordials with Values, Florence	$24.95
3326	**Very Rare Glassware** of the Depression Years, 3rd Series, Florence	$24.95
4732	**Very Rare Glassware** of the Depression Years, 5th Series, Florence	$24.95
4656	**Westmoreland Glass**, Wilson	$24.95

POTTERY

4927	**ABC Plates & Mugs**, Lindsay	$24.95
4929	**American Art Pottery**, Sigafoose	$24.95
4630	**American Limoges**, Limoges	$24.95
1312	**Blue & White Stoneware**, McNerney	$9.95
1958	So. Potteries **Blue Ridge Dinnerware**, 3rd Ed., Newbound	$14.95
1959	**Blue Willow**, 2nd Ed., Gaston	$14.95
4848	Ceramic **Coin Banks**, Stoddard	$19.95
4851	Collectible **Cups & Saucers**, Harran	$18.95
4709	Collectible **Kay Finch**, Biography, Identification & Values, Martinez/Frick	$18.95
1373	Collector's Encyclopedia of **American Dinnerware**, Cunningham	$24.95
4931	Collector's Encyclopedia of **Bauer Pottery**, Chipman	$24.95
3815	Collector's Encyclopedia of **Blue Ridge Dinnerware**, Newbound	$19.95
4932	Collector's Encyclopedia of **Blue Ridge Dinnerware**, Vol. II, Newbound	$24.95
4658	Collector's Encyclopedia of **Brush-McCoy Pottery**, Huxford	$24.95
2272	Collector's Encyclopedia of **California Pottery**, Chipman	$24.95
3811	Collector's Encyclopedia of **Colorado Pottery**, Carlton	$24.95
2133	Collector's Encyclopedia of **Cookie Jars**, Roerig	$24.95
3723	Collector's Encyclopedia of **Cookie Jars**, Book II, Roerig	$24.95
4939	Collector's Encyclopedia of **Cookie Jars**, Book III, Roerig	$24.95
4638	Collector's Encyclopedia of **Dakota Potteries**, Dommel	$24.95
5040	Collector's Encyclopedia of **Fiesta**, 8th Ed., Huxford	$19.95
4718	Collector's Encyclopedia of **Figural Planters & Vases**, Newbound	$19.95
3961	Collector's Encyclopedia of **Early Noritake**, Alden	$24.95
1439	Collector's Encyclopedia of **Flow Blue China**, Gaston	$19.95
3812	Collector's Encyclopedia of **Flow Blue China**, 2nd Ed., Gaston	$24.95
3813	Collector's Encyclopedia of **Hall China**, 2nd Ed., Whitmyer	$24.95
3431	Collector's Encyclopedia of **Homer Laughlin China**, Jasper	$24.95
1276	Collector's Encyclopedia of **Hull Pottery**, Roberts	$19.95
3962	Collector's Encyclopedia of **Lefton China**, DeLozier	$19.95
4855	Collector's Encyclopedia of **Lefton China**, Book II, DeLozier	$19.95
2210	Collector's Encyclopedia of **Limoges Porcelain**, 2nd Ed., Gaston	$24.95
2334	Collector's Encyclopedia of **Majolica Pottery**, Katz-Marks	$19.95
1358	Collector's Encyclopedia of **McCoy Pottery**, Huxford	$19.95
3963	Collector's Encyclopedia of **Metlox Potteries**, Gibbs Jr.	$24.95
3837	Collector's Encyclopedia of **Nippon Porcelain**, Van Patten	$24.95
2089	Collector's Ency. of **Nippon Porcelain**, 2nd Series, Van Patten	$24.95
1665	Collector's Ency. of **Nippon Porcelain**, 3rd Series, Van Patten	$24.95
4712	Collector's Ency. of **Nippon Porcelain**, 4th Series, Van Patten	$24.95
1447	Collector's Encyclopedia of **Noritake**, Van Patten	$19.95
3432	Collector's Encyclopedia of **Noritake**, 2nd Series, Van Patten	$24.95
1037	Collector's Encyclopedia of **Occupied Japan**, 1st Series, Florence	$14.95
1038	Collector's Encyclopedia of **Occupied Japan**, 2nd Series, Florence	$14.95
2088	Collector's Encyclopedia of **Occupied Japan**, 3rd Series, Florence	$14.95
2019	Collector's Encyclopedia of **Occupied Japan**, 4th Series, Florence	$14.95
2335	Collector's Encyclopedia of **Occupied Japan**, 5th Series, Florence	$14.95
4951	Collector's Encyclopedia of **Old Ivory China**, Hillman	$24.95
3964	Collector's Encyclopedia of **Pickard China**, Reed	$24.95
3877	Collector's Encyclopedia of **R.S. Prussia**, 4th Series, Gaston	$24.95
1034	Collector's Encyclopedia of **Roseville Pottery**, Huxford	$19.95
1035	Collector's Encyclopedia of **Roseville Pottery**, 2nd Ed., Huxford	$19.95
4856	Collector's Encyclopeida of **Russel Wright**, 2nd Ed., Kerr	$24.95
4713	Collector's Encyclopedia of **Salt Glaze Stoneware**, Taylor/Lowrance	$24.95
3314	Collector's Encyclopedia of **Van Briggle** Art Pottery, Sasicki	$24.95
4563	Collector's Encyclopedia of **Wall Pockets**, Newbound	$19.95
2111	Collector's Encyclopedia of **Weller Pottery**, Huxford	$29.95
3876	Collector's Guide to **Lu-Ray Pastels**, Meehan	$18.95
3814	Collector's Guide to **Made in Japan** Ceramics, White	$18.95
4646	Collector's Guide to **Made in Japan** Ceramics, Book II, White	$18.95
4565	Collector's Guide to **Rockingham**, The Enduring Ware, Brewer	$14.95
2339	Collector's Guide to **Shawnee Pottery**, Vanderbilt	$19.95

1425	**Cookie Jars**, Westfall	$9.95
3440	**Cookie Jars**, Book II, Westfall	$19.95
4924	Figural & Novelty **Salt & Pepper Shakers**, 2nd Series, Davern	$24.95
2379	Lehner's Ency. of **U.S. Marks** on Pottery, Porcelain & China	$24.95
4722	**McCoy Pottery**, Collector's Reference & Value Guide, Hanson/Nissen	$19.95
3825	**Purinton Pottery**, Morris	$24.95
4726	**Red Wing Art Pottery**, 1920s–1960s, Dollen	$19.95
1670	**Red Wing Collectibles**, DePasquale	$9.95
1440	**Red Wing Stoneware**, DePasquale	$9.95
1632	**Salt & Pepper Shakers**, Guarnaccia	$9.95
5091	**Salt & Pepper Shakers** II, Guarnaccia	$18.95
2220	**Salt & Pepper Shakers** III, Guarnaccia	$14.95
3443	**Salt & Pepper Shakers** IV, Guarnaccia	$18.95
3738	**Shawnee Pottery**, Mangus	$24.95
4629	Turn of the Century **American Dinnerware**, 1880s–1920s, Jasper	$24.95
4572	**Wall Pockets** of the Past, Perkins	$17.95
3327	**Watt Pottery** – Identification & Value Guide, Morris	$19.95

OTHER COLLECTIBLES

4704	Antique & Collectible **Buttons**, Wisniewski	$19.95
2269	Antique **Brass & Copper** Collectibles, Gaston	$16.95
1880	Antique **Iron**, McNerney	$9.95
3872	Antique **Tins**, Dodge	$24.95
4845	Antique **Typewriters & Office Collectibles**, Rehr	$19.95
1714	**Black** Collectibles, Gibbs	$19.95
1128	**Bottle** Pricing Guide, 3rd Ed., Cleveland	$7.95
4636	**Celluloid Collectibles**, Dunn	$14.95
3718	Collectible **Aluminum**, Grist	$16.95
3445	Collectible **Cats**, An Identification & Value Guide, Fyke	$18.95
4560	Collectible **Cats**, An Identification & Value Guide, Book II, Fyke	$19.95
4852	Collectible **Compact Disc** Price Guide 2, Cooper	$17.95
2018	Collector's Encyclopedia of **Granite Ware**, Greguire	$24.95
3430	Collector's Encyclopedia of **Granite Ware**, Book 2, Greguire	$24.95
4705	Collector's Guide to **Antique Radios**, 4th Ed., Bunis	$18.95
3880	Collector's Guide to **Cigarette Lighters**, Flanagan	$17.95
4637	Collector's Guide to **Cigarette Lighers**, Book II, Flanagan	$17.95
4942	Collector's Guide to **Don Winton Designs**, Ellis	$19.95
3966	Collector's Guide to **Inkwells**, Identification & Values, Badders	$18.95
4947	Collector's Guide to **Inkwells**, Book II, Badders	$19.95
4948	Collector's Guide to **Letter Openers**, Grist	$19.95
4862	Collector's Guide to **Toasters** & Accessories, Greguire	$19.95
4652	Collector's Guide to **Transistor Radios**, 2nd Ed., Bunis	$16.95
4653	Collector's Guide to **TV Memorabilia**, 1960s–1970s, Davis/Morgan	$24.95
4864	Collector's Guide to **Wallace Nutting Pictures**, Ivankovich	$18.95
1629	**Doorstops**, Identification & Values, Bertoia	$9.95
4567	Figural **Napkin Rings**, Gottschalk & Whitson	$18.95
4717	Figural **Nodders**, Includes Bobbin' Heads and Swayers, Irtz	$19.95
3968	**Fishing Lure** Collectibles, Murphy/Edmisten	$24.95
4867	**Flea Market Trader**, 11th Ed., Huxford	$9.95
4944	**Flue Covers**, Collector's Value Guide, Meckley	$12.95
4945	**G-Men and FBI Toys** and Collectibles, Whitworth	$18.95
5043	**Garage Sale & Flea Market Annual**, 6th Ed.	$19.95
3819	**General Store Collectibles**, Wilson	$24.95
4643	**Great American West** Collectibles, Wilson	$24.95
2215	Goldstein's **Coca-Cola** Collectibles	$16.95
3884	Huxford's Collectible **Advertising**, 2nd Ed.	$24.95
2216	**Kitchen Antiques**, 1790–1940, McNerney	$14.95
4950	The **Lone Ranger**, Collector's Reference & Value Guide, Felbinger	$18.95
2026	**Railroad** Collectibles, 4th Ed., Baker	$14.95
4949	**Schroeder's Antiques Price Guide**, 16th Ed., Huxford	$12.95
5007	**Silverplated Flatware**, Revised 4th Edition, Hagan	$18.95
1922	Standard **Old Bottle** Price Guide, Sellari	$14.95
4708	Summers' Guide to **Coca-Cola**	$19.95
4952	Summers' Pocket Guide to **Coca-Cola** Identifications	$9.95
3892	**Toy & Miniature Sewing Machines**, Thomas	$18.95
4876	**Toy & Miniature Sewing Machines**, Book II, Thomas	$24.95
3828	Value Guide to **Advertising Memorabilia**, Summers	$18.95
3977	Value Guide to **Gas Station** Memorabilia, Summers & Priddy	$24.95
4877	Vintage **Bar Ware**, Visakay	$24.95
4935	The W.F. Cody **Buffalo Bill** Collector's Guide with Values	$24.95
4879	**Wanted to Buy**, 6th Edition	$9.95

This is only a partial listing of the books on antiques that are available from Collector Books. All books are well illustrated and contain current values. Most of these books are available from your local bookseller, antique dealer, or public library. If you are unable to locate certain titles in your area, you may order by mail from COLLECTOR BOOKS, P.O. Box 3009, Paducah, KY 42002-3009. Customers with Visa, Discover or MasterCard may phone in orders from 7:00–5:00 CST, Monday–Friday, Toll Free 1-800-626-5420. Add $2.00 for postage for the first book ordered and $0.30 for each additional book. Include item number, title, and price when ordering. Allow 14 to 21 days for delivery.